Buy Golly!

Buy Golly!

Cover picture

Merrythought Glove Golly

1967

First published in the UK by

New Cavendish Books

3 Denbigh Road, London W11 2SJ

T: (44) 207 229 6765, (44) 207 792 9984

F: (44) 207 792 0027

W: www.newcavendishbooks.co.uk

E: sales@newcavendishbooks.co.uk

Design by Peter Cope

ISBN 1 872727 28 X

Printed and bound in Thailand by
Sirivatana Interprint Public Co., Ltd.

Contents

Illustrator: Charles Folkard

From *The Land of Nursery Rhyme*

Published by Dent Dutton

1932

Foreword

In researching the origins of the golliwog and writing this book
I have endeavoured to be as objective as as possible.
The golliwog's links with slavery and racial prejudice may prove to be
unpalatable and uncomfortable to some, though I stand by my every word.
My affection for the golliwog is not based purely on artistic appreciation,
but derives from love and respect for my culture and its historical associations.
Everyone has their reasons for loving or disliking golliwogs and
we should recognise that we are all entitled to our own opinions.

Sincerely, Clinton Derricks

Preface

To capture the childhood of the country ....
to poison its early understanding of history
by false ideals and pseudo-heroes .... to feed the
always overweening pride of race ....
to fasten this base insularity of mind and
morals upon the little children of a nation and
to call it patriotism is as foul an abuse
of education as it is possible to conceive.
J A Hobson, *Imperialism: A Study,* 1902.

The coming of the golliwog

The first nigger doll of note to feature in English literature was *The Golliwogg*, a character who appeared in *The Adventures of Two Dutch Dolls* created by Florence Upton. It was the first of a series of thirteen volumes published between 1895 and 1909 and was heralded with a great deal of press acclaim. So popular was *The Golliwogg* in English nurseries that it was his name and not the Dutch Dolls that appeared in the title of every subsequent volume. Children loved him – he was indeed 'the prince of golliwogs'. *The Golliwogg*, while adventurous and daring, was impeccably behaved and well mannered, always treating his companions courteously.

However, *The Golliwogg's* arrival prompted a flood of material featuring golliwogs and negros, much of which was created by less discerning, commercially driven artists and writers.

At the turn of the 20th century there was a burgeoning market for colour picture books, magazines and masses of picture postcards and greetings cards. The Empire was at its zenith and people were having a wonderful time in Edwardian Britain. Artists and writers, free from the strictures of Victorian times, could express themselves freely, but this often meant making fun at the expense of the black man.

A climate of racial prejudice

Racial prejudice was endemic in Victorian and Edwardian Britain, affecting young and old alike. Many school books, stories and other material created for children and young adults, were tarnished with institutionalised racism. In his book, *Victorian Juvenilia and the Image of the Black African*, [1975-76], Jake W Spidle observes that in the adventure stories written by the likes of RM Ballantyne, GA Henty, WHG Kingston, Frederick Marryat, Thomas Mayne Reid and William Stables, blacks are repeatedly portrayed as lazy, grotesque, ignorant, incapable of complex thinking, tearful, foolish, thieves and liars. These attitudes, repeated over and over again, distorted perceptions until stereotypes and myths about black people were accepted as reality.

The following quotations and remarks were made by prominent and respected members of society. Today, it is astonishing to think these views were universally condoned.

"The Negroes are made on purpose to serve the whites, just as the black ants are made on purpose to serve the red." Thomas Carlyle and Anthony Trollope. *The Spectator*, 1865.

"We are face to face with barbarous peoples, whom it is profitless to conquer, yet amongst whom it is difficult otherwise to enforce peace and order! This difficulty meets every nation which goes forth to carry civilisation amongst uncivilised peoples." The Class History of England, Cassell & Co, 1884.

"The highest places in the hierarchy of civilisation will assuredly not be within the reach of our dusky cousins." TH Huxley in *The Reader*, 1865.

"The Negro has not yet attained to the elevation of character necessary to sustain the higher order of family life." A Caldecott in *Society for Promoting Christian Knowledge*, 1889.

"Monkeys were far more civilised than these naked savages. Never saw such scoundrels as Africa produces. Quite on a level with that of the brute and not to be compared with the noble character of the dog." Anthropologist, Edward B Tyler

"Niggers are like monkeys. It is not only their subnormal sloping foreheads and large protruding lips. They sit about in the streets and babble like monkeys; always pinching and playing tricks." GW Stevens in *The Land of the Dollar*, 1897.

Empire meant to build an authority of the English-speaking race over the dark-skinned myriads of Africa and Asia." Last will and testament of Cecil John Rhodes in *Reviews of Reviews*, 1902.

"The Negro is best described as an over grown child, vain, self-indulgent and fond of idleness, but with a good heart .... Life is so easy to him in his native home that he has never developed the qualities of industry, self-denial, and forethought .... the negroes have never got united in a strong and stable kingdom. He lives in a hut built of mud, reeds, or grasses and wears little or no clothing" Thomas Nelson, in *The World and its People*, 1903.

"Because the British ruled blacks, they have a duty to increase the moral and educational progress of the child-like natives." Sir Charles Eliot in *The East African Protectorate*, 1905.

"Blacks were, lazy, vicious, and incapable of any serious improvement, or of work except under compulsion. In such a climate a few bananas will sustain the life of a negro quite sufficiently." Rudyard Kipling *School History of England*, 1911.

"Nigger children, like baby camels, baby wild boars, and baby giraffes, are among the prettiest creatures in the world." *Daily Mail* journalist, Hugh Edward Egerton in *British Colonial Policy in the 20th Century* 1922.

Misuse of the caricature

New forms of colour printing enabled artists to exploit the caricature and create expressive, colourful and humorous renderings of people. However, caricatures of black men soon became stereotyped – round eyes, thick lips, fuzzy hair, broad grins and a happy-go-lucky manner. Fuelled by a society riven with racial prejudice, many journeyman artists poked fun at the black man with crass and degrading humour. They were egged on by commercial expediency and employer pressure – "You're good at these, they're popular, do more, get paid". Many decades would have to pass before there was a strong enough anti-racist lobby to put a stop to this reckless disregard for black people.

Illustration for a postcard design by William Henry Ellam for W Mack, London, (unpublished), c.1920. (Collection: Peter Cope)

Questions of race

These questions are typical of those I am asked about my attitude in relation to the golliwog and its racial connotations.

Q: "Don't you think you are too supersensitive concerning the golliwog, looking for insults where none were intended?"
A: To those people I simply say, "Continue studying this book".

Q: "Surely, there was never any racist intention with this character. It is an enchanting fantasy?".
A: We cannot dismiss these stereotypes as fantasy, when nearly every depiction of blacks in the 19th century was positioned in this same demeaning way. So much so, that black people still find it difficult to shake free of these grotesque images for more positive figures. Just take a look at some of the illustrations in this book and see how you would feel if portrayed in a similar way.

Q: "Don't you think many whites loved the golliwog and saw no connection with people of colour?"
A: This is true. There were some owners of golliwogs, who saw no reflection of black people, but I believe many more did! It is difficult for me to see it any other way when, before and during the 19th century the colour and word 'black' had negative connotations. Black was a term lending itself to evil, something scary and to be mocked. Black people were looked upon in this way and there is no denying it was a very popular attitude in white western society. Some writers who wanted their books published jumped on this bandwagon and rode to fame and fortune. Furthermore, just as there were those who loved golliwogs, there were others who loved the idea of servitude and slavery and saw nothing unacceptable about it.

Q: "Don't you agree that golly stories and toys should not be taken so seriously as to warrant the use of such emotive accusations as racist. After all, they are only make-believe and children love them."
A: Naturally, blacks are hurt by any assault on their physical or spiritual being, whether illustrated, written or spoken. Some white children were, and still are, encouraged to hold people of other race or colour in disregard. Filling young, impressionable minds with images reflecting black people in a poor light preserves a notion leading to prejudice.

Q: "Why are blacks so sensitive? Surely there wouldn't be a problem if the protagonist was white and was caricatured in a grotesque fashion?"
A: Of course there would be no problem. From an early age a white child assumes with confidence the mantle of inheritor of the greatest achievements of humankind and does not feel threatened.

Q: "It is dangerous to censor children's books, there is no telling where it will stop. Surely, children should not be denied the chance to read their favourite golliwog and sambo stories?"
A: Good books and toys feed the imagination, and stimulate the reader's mind. Bad books, some of which might hold up to ridicule the black face, simply perpetuate prejudice.

Taking coals to Newcastle!

In February 1990, the London *Evening Standard* reported that *"a British toy firm which sells hand made golliwogs to Harrods has won a lucrative order – to supply them to Africa.*

The golly, often regarded as a symbol of racist oppression attracted a Nigerian buyer at the Earls Court toy fair. He placed a £5000.00 export order with the firm Cornish Fairies *of Helston, Cornwall. The firm will send a consignment to a store in Lagos with the emphasis on gollies and other black dolls."*

Enid Blyton in the dock

Popular children's writers such as Enid Blyton and Hugh Lofting were guilty of deplorable representation of black people in their books. Lofting, whose *Doctor Dolittle* stories cast black people as grotesque, when a little girl is scared by 'a horrible, dreadful [black] face', while in Blyton's *Five Fall into Adventure*, we encounter a character 'with nasty gleaming eyes, and it looked very dark – perhaps it was a black man's face!' In *The Little Black Doll*, the doll's face, being black, is a disgrace and needs to be erased in order to be approved by the other toys. When it is washed and becomes pink, it becomes "a nice looking doll...as good as any other".

A landmark case arose in the late 1960s highlighting public sensitivity to racial issues, when Enid Blyton's *Here Comes Noddy Again* came in for a great deal of criticism from the anti-racist lobby. The storyline portrayed Noddy being mugged in a dark wood by golliwogs, who made off with his car and clothing. The story has since been revised using other characters after pressure from many quarters.

During the 1960s many such negative examples continued to be published and are eagerly sought by collectors today.

Are golliwogs banned in Britain nowadays?

There is a popular belief that the sale of gollies and golliwog-related material is banned in Britain. Although golliwogs appear less in children's books these days, they are not banned.

In August 1981, a correspondent in the *Times Diary* noted, *"The imminent demise of the long-threatened golliwog was confirmed yesterday by the* Toy Manufacturers Association. *Conservation measures have failed in the face of prolonged sniping by social equality groups and now only 2,500* [golliwogs] *a year are sold in toy shops compared with up to 200,000 when the species was in demand after the war. The decline has been accentuated since the* National Committee on Racism in Children's Books *decided that golliwogs 'reinforced harmful stereotypes in children' and launched a campaign which was supported by the* Commission for Racial Equality."

The following comments made in January 1987 by *The Times* newspaper, reflect the change in social attitudes that have reduced the number of golliwogs to be seen in children's literature during the latter part of the 20th century:

"Golliwogs may have been OK 40 years ago but are not appropriate in a multi-racial society. They are gross caricatures of black people and are offensive to them."

In the beginning

Why write a book on golliwogs?

This book has been written to preserve the history of one of Great Britain's most popular toys during the late 19th and early 20th centuries – the golliwog. The golliwog is now over 100 years old. Created in 1895, this fascinating and somewhat controversial character has delighted and amused many children and adults. No one could have ever imagined that this black rag doll, thought to look 'horrid' by some parents, would be so popular. As a result of its popularity, over the last one hundred years a myriad of publishers, manufacturers and advertisers have produced countless items bearing the golliwog's likeness attesting to its immense success.

This is a reference, not only for those just starting their golliwog collection, but for the seasoned collector as well. With the upsurge of 'gollimania' among enthusiasts we need to explore the social history surrounding golliwogs; examine attitudes towards its imagery and impact; present the variety of dolls and other items produced; and assist enthusiasts with 'correct' data on their collections. A collector who is informed of specific details such as manufacturers, production year, materials used, design pinpointing, desirability, etc, is able to decide wisely whether or not to secure an item.

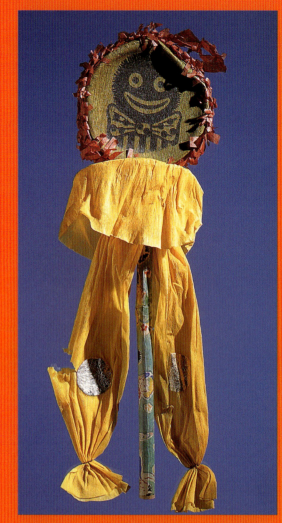

Party rattle, English, 1920s

Porcelain Golliwog and Dutch doll, possibly by Rudolstadt or Huebach Germany, 1925

Child's tray, English, 1930s

Right: Child's egg-cup (golliwog at cricket), English, 1930s

Below: Child's mug, Shell Pottery with Butcher's transfers, English, 1920s

Right: Baby's plate (Johnson Ltd), English, 1920s

Left: Child's mug (golliwog at cricket), English, 1930s

Far left: Postcard by Agnes Richardson, English, 1930s

Below: Child's mug, possibly by Huebach or Rudolstadt, Germany, 1907

What is a golliwog?

At first, the golliwog was a gnome whose image was modelled on the dehumanised minstrels of the early 19th century.

It is thought that the first illustration of a golliwog is to be found in the work of Florence Upton who used dolls and toys she owned as models for the characters in her books. Among these was an old minstrel doll given to her as a child while she was living in America. This doll was the model for the first golliwog. It now resides in the Museum of Childhood, Bethnal Green in London.

The popularity of minstrel shows during the mid-18th to early 20th centuries in America, England and Europe paved the way and created the demand for black dolls, stories and toys. These playthings and literary characters were created for the predominantly moneyed white consumer and many cruel and grotesque images were produced. Originating in the USA, these characters became even more popular when boosted by Britain's *Black Sambo* and *Golliwogg*, the latter of which is the subject of this book.

The minstrel was the original and continuing form for the golliwog in Great Britain. In 1895, Florence Upton along with her mother Bertha, created a book for children entitled, *The Adventures of Two Dutch Dolls* in which the golliwog was a featured character. So popular was the book that 12 other volumes followed, with the golliwog as the main attraction.

Soon after the initial book appeared, toy companies and other publishers began to create their versions of the golliwog, the earliest doll selling at Gamages department store in 1902. The Uptons, like Helen Bannerman, (author of *Little Black Sambo*) filed no copyright for their creation, thus, as with Sambo giving artists, authors, toy companies and advertisers free range to create their own portrayals of these characters.

Underground poster, 1928 by British artist, Austin Cooper. Designed for a public service announcement. The golliwog's colours are red, white and blue. Size: 39 x 25 inches.

No.2. **Stockinette Nigger.** Covers entire head. Price **5/6** Post 2d.

No.3. **Minstrel Mask** Stockinette, covers head. Price **5/9** Ditto. Face mask only **1/9**. Post 2d.

Three masks from a 1913 Gamages catalogue

SHOP BY UNDERGROUND BUT SHOP BY UNDERGROUND BETWEEN 10 & 4

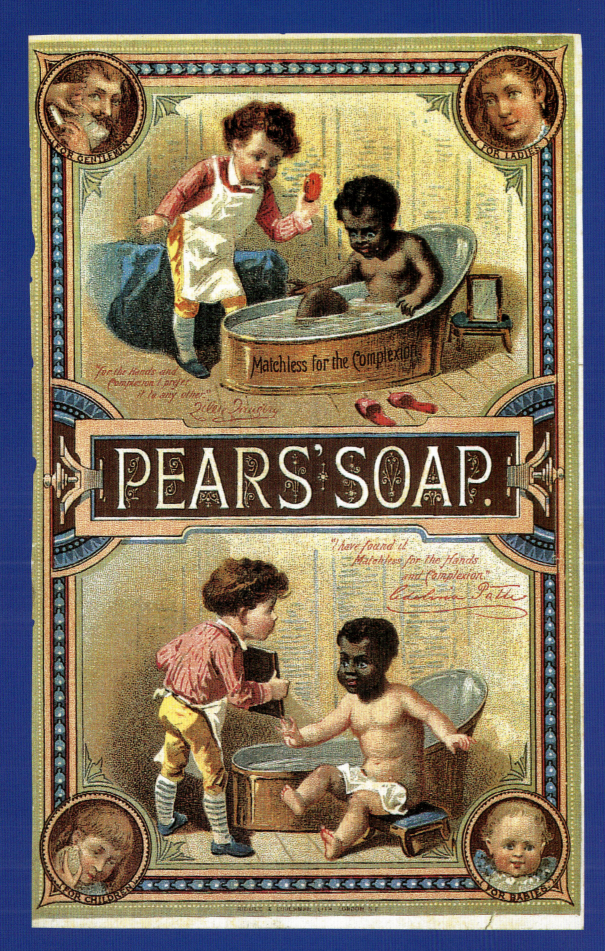

Pears' Soap advertisement
English, early 1900s

*Ashtray or card stand
with twin golliwogs,
painted wood, 37 inches
high, 1920s*

*Greetings card by
Raphael Tuck & Sons,
English, 1890s*

What's in a name?

What is the origin of the name 'golliwog'? Is it 'pollywog' (a tadpole with a large head and tapered tail) or 'Wog' (jargon for (Western Oriental Gentleman), or Wogs (working on government service), sometimes descriptive of 'coloureds' in government employ in Africa and India. No one is sure, just as no one knows who made the first golliwog doll. Dolls of this type were made in America in in the early days, popularly tagged with different names, like 'mumbo' dolls, 'nigger' dolls, etc.).

I have decided to accept Florence Upton's account: *"He fell into our hands when we were children. He came from an American Fair, and in those days he was nameless. I picked him up in my studio, and without even the idea of a name passing through my head. I called him Golliwogg"*.

Initially, white parents were concerned that the golliwog would frighten their children. On the contrary, children loved the character, which surprised many parents. Adults often overlook the fact that any character, no matter how 'grotesque', can win a child's heart, if it is kind, loving, brave, funny and takes children on a mental and emotional adventure. A case in point is the film ET. Rarely have we seen a character more 'grotesque' than the little extra-terrestrial trying to get home. His efforts created an adventure involving the neighbourhood children. Needless to say ET was a huge success! In 1910 the golliwog craze was fueled when Robertson, the jam company, adopted the character as its trademark. Its promotional campaigns helped to make the golliwog part of the British tradition. The character's popularity was at its peak during the early 1900s and many golliwog items were produced to meet growing demand. Around 1918 the spelling was changed to 'golliwog' or 'golly-wog', while Robertsons used the term 'golly' from its slogan, 'golly it's good'. Many golliwog toys, books, and dolls were made in Britain at that time and in 1913 Germany offered its first 'Gow' (a version of the golliwog) doll made of felt and leather. Golliwogs, like teddy bears, gave boys and girls a doll friend to play with and confide in without feeling uncomfortable.

*Robertsons placard
(cardboard), 20 x 30 inches,
1970s*

*Child's Christmas
handkerchief with
golliwogs on each corner,
c. 1910*

*Pair of golliwog salt &
pepper shakers
British, c.1950s*

The war years

During World War I many toy firms were
involved in the war effort. There were also
trading embargoes against Germany, which
opened the door for new companies to begin
producing soft toys in Britain, many of them
featuring golliwogs in their line of products.
The first golliwogs made between 1903 and
1925 had noses like the Florence Upton
original. Around 1930 Robertsons, changed
the look of its 'golly', as the nose made the
character look too grotesque. Soon other
companies followed.

The face became flat in appearance and
has remained so even today with very few
exceptions. Materials which were used were
also changing around this time. The
golliwogs made from 1900 to the mid 1920s
were filled with either a mixture of wood-
wool, cork, horsehair, flock or cotton.
During the late 1920s, kapok, a fine cotton
taken from the seed pod of the *Ceiba pent-
andra* tree, was the most popular material
used into the early 1930s. It was initially
used to stuff lifejackets and cushions.

Other materials such as quality velvets,
linens, satins, silks, cottons and fur were
used from 1900 to early 1930s. Linen disc
and wooden boot buttons were commonly
used for eyes during this period. Later,
during the mid-1930s and up to the early
1950s celluloid, paint, felt or oilcloth were
employed as eyes, while many synthetic
fabrics were used for the clothing. Foam was
the most popular stuffing for all soft toys.
Eventually sailcloth, velveteen, cotton plush
and other synthetic materials became
popular at the beginning of the 1960s and
right up to the present. (9)

World War II caused many toy
companies to cease their toy making
activities and assist the war effort. Most of
the materials mentioned earlier were used
and rationed for the war. Sadly, many of the
soft toys were lost, discarded or used for
dressing. It is no wonder they are so rare!
These early golliwogs now command high
prices for their quality, scarcity and history.

Birthday card, English, 1940s

Myra A Gavino design for Serendipity Child's Cothing bag, 1980s

Below right: Child's dish, 'British Anchor Pottery' English, 1920s

The post-war years

After the World War II, sales figures for the golliwog declined. The 1950s brought new characters from books to television, exciting TV programming plus movie heroes as well as television character toys. All were now produced with the new 'plastics'. Also, more interesting toys and dolls were being produced, thus reflecting the boom of the post war era: toy soldiers, glamour dolls, battery-operated cars, planes, boats and even science fiction toys. No golliwog could compete with all this. Finally, there was a decline in the birth rate and with the influx of cheaper imported merchandise from the East, many of the soft toy makers went out of business. Countries such as China, Korea and Taiwan had very low production costs and manufactured a never-ending stream of cheap imitations.

Golliwogs abroad

Although Britain was the major producer of golliwogs, they were also made abroad, particularly in America and Australia.

Today, the only major company in Britain making golliwogs is Merrythought. There are a few small firms in Britain and around the world producing golliwog merchandise and a number of bear and doll artists making the odd golliwog doll, but a more multicultural society and a greater sensitivity to race and colour has led many companies and artists to refrain from creating golliwog dolls or toys.

The Dinah Doll, *Dean's Knockabout Toy Sheet* Pub: Dean's Rag Book Co, 1906. Collection Peter & Dawn Cope

Assembling a golliwog collection

When you set out to build a golliwog collection you should first establish the amount of capital, time, and space you can commit. There are many types of golliwog items which occasionally surface in the collecting arena, and your budget will play an important part in deciding which pieces to secure. I recommend you buy what appeals to you, items which you would enjoy living with. Avoid buying for investment only, as the climate may be favourable at the time of purchase, but six months later the market could wane.

Look for the best examples available. Those in poor condition should be avoided unless they are extremely rare. Mundane items have a tendency to turn up regularly, and these should be in good to excellent condition if you should choose to buy. Decide if you wish to have a general or more specialised collection. Some people desire golliwog dolls, others collect books or advertising badges. If you are unsure about how to begin, visit bear, doll or toy fairs, as well as shops and museums.

Talk to dealers or experts at auction houses and read books on the subject but do beware, for some of the information available in books and auction catalogues is incorrect. Still, the more you study the subject, the better you will get to know what to look out for. Popular maybe, but golliwogs were not made or sold to the same extent as teddy bears. You won't come across them as often as other dolls or toys. There may be long periods when these items seem totally unavailable, but if you persevere opportunities to buy will present themselves.

Above: Pinkus & Dove
golliwog jumper. c.1980

Above right: 'Corgi' golliwog
jumper. British. c.1960s

Right: Ring-toss game,
originally made in England,
as seen in the Fancy Toy
Trader, 1915. Subsequently
copied by other companies

Far right: Golliwog brooch,
Wood, British, c.1960s

Evaluating golliwog dolls and toys

To decide the value of a golliwog item, you should consider type, condition, quality, age, size and most of all, its desirability in the market place. The more you collect, the more your appreciation will be honed as you become more aware and increasingly particular. Avoid paying enormous sums of money for collectables unless you can classify them as authentic. For instance, a doll with a manufacturer's label or mark is worth more than the exact same doll that has lost its mark or label.

Detailing and craftsmanship can also affect prices of dolls produced by the same company because of the variation in quality. Quantity can influence prices as well. If a firm produces one article in large quantities, and makes another item in a smaller quantity, the latter is likely to be more valuable. For example, The Dean's Rag Book Company produced a range of golliwogs from 1965 to 1983, all made of sailcloth and all with traditional black faces. In 1966 they created a white faced version called *Mr Smith* but in a limited quantity (about 100), most of which went to the United States of America. Such dolls are rare and the price will reflect their scarcity.

*Left: Combex golliwogs
Squeak toy (rubber)
British, 7 inches, c.1950s*

*Below left: Plastic (also rubber)
golliwog jointed doll,
Hong Kong, 7 inches, c.1960s*

Let the buyer beware

In general, collectors should beware of the occasional unscrupulous dealer. Because of the resurgence of popularity in golliwogs in the collector's market, some dealers and collectors willingly take advantage of those who are inexperienced or poorly informed. Arm yourself with knowledge and always try to get a money back guarantee! Quite often I have examined a golliwog which was clearly made in the 1960s and the dealer would state *It's from the 1940s* or *It's 1920's*. When I corrected them and disclosed my knowledge of the item, they responded with, *Well, that's what I was told!* or *Oh really!*. On a particular occasion, a dealer was selling a 1980s Nisbet golliwog with a Merrythought label crudely attached to its foot and said, *It's a very rare, early doll*. I was annoyed and just walked away. Later I smiled at her desperation in trying to make a fast buck.

You won't find this sort of practice with most dealers but it does exist. Do not be afraid to ask questions and seek advice from other dealers.

Refrain from buying golliwog items in poor condition, unless you like the item and wish to keep it for your own collection, or, the object is so rare that you may never discover another like it. In either case, get the best price you can, and especially if it is a soft doll. Remember, that dolls of this type, unless they are extremely well produced, suffer from age deterioration, or moth attack and will corrode even further, which could affect your investment. Well produced golliwog dolls in poor condition can last another life time if properly cared for. The one thing you must remember is that these items were made to be played with so expect a degree of deterioration. Also, you will find that in some cases that the 'played with' look adds to the character of the doll or toy.

Characteristics of the golliwog

As a rule of thumb, the trade tends to pidgeon-hole golliwog dolls and toys into the following categories or periods.

1. Vintage: 1896 - 1925
2. Early: 1926 - 1945
3. Revival: 1945 - 1966
4. Late: 1967 - present

Early golliwogs dolls usually had noses. Even in 1910, when Robertson's adopted the golliwog as their trademark, he was given a nose. But by the 1930s, the nose was gone, making the golliwog look less human and more gnome-like in appearance. It is hard to find golliwog items with noses nowadays, especially the early or vintage variety; most are in the hands of collectors or still held by their original owners for sentimental reasons. Golliwog dolls and toys, never as popular as teddy bears and other dolls, sold 200,000 a year when they were in demand, but by 1981 only about 2,500 per year were sold. Many were destroyed in the two world wars and the controversy over racism

in the late 1960s caused many to be thrown away. It is fair to add that many golliwog items are now in American, European and Japanese collections, so many in fact, that even British doll and toy dealers are having trouble finding examples. However, if you persevere the chances are that some highly prized examples will come your way.

Most early golliwogs not only had noses, having been modelled on Florence Upton's Golliwogg, they were also clothed in gentlemen's morning dress or similar Victorian costume. Mass produced, some looked rather crudely made, but closer inspection reveals the machine quality and craftsmanship of these dolls. Eyes were made of materials such as cloth, wooden shoe buttons, glass and metal buttons. Real fur was applied as hair and mohair was used for later dolls. They were stuffed with cotton or wood-wool, the latter giving a hard compositional feeling and covered with fabrics, including heavy linens, velvets and satinette. The construction process, partially carried out by hand, gives many early period golliwog dolls their home made and individual appearance.

Opposite:

Far left: Golliwog match striker.
Made by Schäfer & Vater,
Porcelain, c.1900s

Centre: Hard plastic golliwog,
British, c.1950s

Above left: Eb & Flo brooch by
Roden & Son. British, 1940s
Kellogs NSR Co Ltd golliwog
brooch, British, 1966

Left: Originally a 'Dr Dolittle'
doll. The head and hands
were changed then sold as a
1920s doll. I purchased it as an
example of deception

Bottom left: A page from Ten
Little Niggers, British, 1957

Far left: Golliwog teething
rings. 1. Silver, British, 1972.
2. Silver-plated brass, British,
c.1930s

Centre left: Wind-up toy,
Origin unknown, c.1930s

Left: Talke-Hill Pottery,
Golliwog bank, British, c.1920s

Centre far left: Best English
China, Child's dish based on
the Upton books, c.1906

Centre left: Golliwog bank,
China. British. 4^{1}/$_{2}$ inches,
c.1950s

Below left: Three postcards,
1. By Ethel Parkinson,
 Pub. CW Faulkner, c.1912
2. British, c.1913
3. British, c.1923

Below: Celluloid golliwog,
Japanese, c.1920s

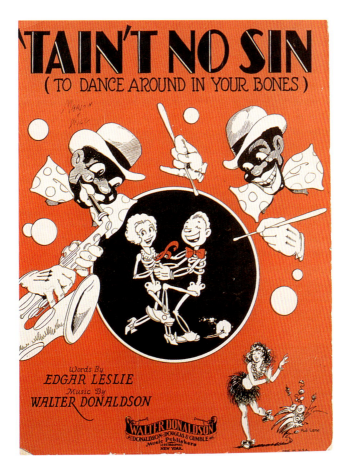

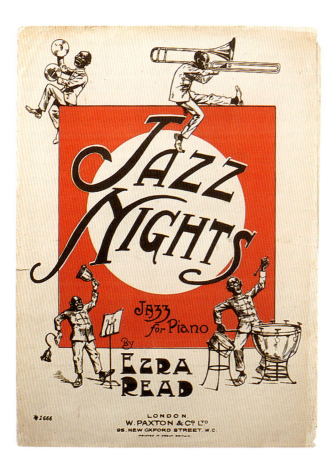

Who collects golliwogs and other black images?

Many collectors of golliwogs and other black related items maintain a discreetly low profile about their collections for obvious reasons. To own these objects, is still considered by many (black and white alike) not to be socially acceptable. So, to avoid the stigma of being racially motivated against people of colour, these items are kept under wraps, only to be viewed in private by close friends and family. While many other toy and doll collectors, boast of the prizes they have obtained, publicly and without any adverse repercussion, collectors of golliwogs and black memorabilia tend to carry their purchases away concealed, to avoid offending anyone. It has been no surprise to me to have experienced great difficulty in locating collectors of these treasures. But now, with these objects making an entry into the collector's market and fetching quite high prices, many collectors are making themselves known.

During my research, I was surprised to hear from one source that eighty per cent of the collectors of black memorabilia in America are black people. In my view this is an exaggeration borne out by the fact that most of the material written on the subject is by white people, who have become the so-called authorities on the subject of black memorabilia. Furthermore, very few blacks attend doll, toy or collectors fairs or visit antique shops. These events and venues are organised and attended largely by whites, so much so, that when I attend, I feel very much in the minority. This holds true in America as it does in Britain and Europe.

In the main, black people like to collect the more positive or contemporary objects of their culture, such as art by black artists, African art and literature about black history. Only a small minority collect toys, dolls or negative imagery. Although more and more blacks have attended fleamarkets in America in recent years, possibly with a view to acquiring black memorabilia, most of the material has already fallen into the hands of other collectors.

Below: 'Le Golliwog' by Vigny. The bottle on the left was made in the 1930s. It has a plastic top with a printed paper face attached. The centre bottle is the second of the series of designs made in 1919. The stopper is made of blue glass which looks black and is topped with seal fur for hair. The bottle on the right contains cologne in the head of a glass. All are made in France by Verreries Brosse. There was also a perfume pin with the golliwog head only.

The centre bottles (very scarce) were designed by Michael de Brunhoff in 1917, around the time when Gaby Deglys toured Europe with the first black jazz band. This first bottle had a black glass stopper, representing the face and hair. The other bottles (with fur) were also designed by de Brunhoff. Other golliwog bottles were made by Baccarat (not shown).

Contrary to popular belief, Lalique did not make the golliwog bottles for Vigny. Only three perfume bottles were made for Vigny, by Lalique: Ambre Jamerose and Musky.

Right: Postcard, FG Lewin, 1922

Far right: Postcard, c.1920s

*Below left: Postcard,
Arnold Taylor. c.1930s*

*Below centre: Postcard.
FG Lewin, 1922*

Below right: Postcard, 1929

For many years blacks rejected these images, wanting nothing to do with them. Now that many black people are aware of their true history and have acquired greater confidence and self-esteem, they are able to take a more objective view and experience shows that many black collectors come from an arts or education background. Some blacks collect golliwogs and black memorabilia because, like it or not, it is a part of their culture and others have come to find beauty in these traditional representations. However, there are still many black people who want nothing to do with golliwogs or any negative reflections of their past and wish to rid the market of this type of imagery.

So why do white people like to collect these impressions of black culture? The thought of golliwogs and associated toys triggers fond memories of childhood for the vast majority of collectors. Golliwogs were soft and cuddly characters, there to be taken on adventures or to share loving secrets with. If we'd stopped to think, we may have been curious about our golly's origins, but in those naïve and carefree days, people recognised no adverse connection between black people and golliwogs, less still servitude, particularly in a society where even middle class families still employed live-in servants, almost all of whom were white.

Of course, there are those with no affinity whatsoever with golliwogs, but who speculate in the market and expect to make large profits from the sale of their investments.

Most people who collect dolls, books, toys, or anything from their childhood days, do so for the sheer joy of that nostalgic journey where the sun always shines and they can retreat from the harshness of life in today's real world.

Above: 'The Nigger Cap' (racist party cap). 'Be a Nigger, then, return a white man, German, early 1900s

Right: Wizard comics, 1940

The minstrel

To understand fully the impact and image of golliwogs, we must first explore the 19th century period in America, prior to the publication of Florence Upton's 'Golliwogg' books, a series that brought golliwogs to the fore in children's nurseries. Before and after the American Civil War, there were black rag dolls made to look like mammies, servants and field hands. Various materials were used to make them: wood, corn husk, nutshells, clay, dried fruit, leather and straw, but old used rags were the most common. These dolls were made by black slaves and white slave owners alike. The only toy doll a black child would have was probably such a rag doll. Their parents would not have been able to afford any of the toys in the shops, so with leftover material, thread and buttons, family members would make the dolls, for the young girls and boys.

All dolls carry with them a part of history. It is said that black rag dolls were used as a means of smuggling messages, medicine and bandages to confederate soldiers during the Civil War.

An early handmade nigger doll, American, c.1870s

Right and opposite: Three die-cut figures, British, c.1890s-1900s

Opposite above: Lithographs published by W Spooner, British, c.1880s

A doll would be carried through enemy lines, supposedly destined for a young girl, but on reaching its destination, usually a military camp, soldiers would find their needs concealed inside its body. The Yankees never suspected a black toy or doll might carry contraband. If they saw them, they thought it was a taunt to remind them of the reason why the war was being fought.

After the war, black rag dolls assumed fancier clothing and accessories as blacks began to advance in the socio-economic structure. But there were still many rag dolls attired in poor quality clothing, well into the 20th century. Toy manufacturers began producing black rag dolls after noting their popularity in the late 19th century. Various methods were used to create these dolls. In the 1830s Izannah Walker used a hand press to mould the faces and bodies of her cloth dolls, Leo Moss used papier-maché for his creations in the late 19th century and Rosa Wildes Blackman chose clay to model the heads of her rag dolls. Others had the cloth printed with a 'likeness' of a black face, mostly used as advertising for food and other products.

Rag dolls on which golliwogs were based, are the handmade cloth dolls of the middle and late 1800s with embroidered or attached features. It was such a doll, given to Florence Upton as a child, which she used as the model for of the first golliwog characters in literature.

Minstrel – any of a troupe of performers usually with blackened faces, giving a performance of supposedly Negro singing, jokes, dances, etc. *Penguin English Dictionary* 1985-1986.

Possibly the first black characters or performers to become famous in America, Great Britain and Europe were the Minstrel Troupes – white performers who counterfeited black culture. Unknown to these players, they were echoing blacks, who were themselves imitating complacency on the plantation.

Long before the American Revolution of 1860, whites were blackening their faces to mimic black people as entertainment. Always depicted as barbarians or buffoons, black people were constantly perceived as less than human – 'mere animals'. During the eighteenth century, artists of America, Great Britain, and Europe contributed to the racial myths constructed on differences in skin colour and physical attributes of 'inferior' peoples. Such myths were used to justify the Christianisation and 'liberation' of such peoples.

Around the 1820s when slavery was exposed to criticism and revolt by Abolitionists and slaves alike, white entertainers travelling around America in black face were performing what they called 'real' Negro songs and dances. I can imagine just how absurd they appeared, because when I observe whites imitating black voices, movement and dress, it always appears excessive. Many blacks (who pretend to laugh but are not really amused), find such blatant mimicry (which is especially popular among white males) offensive. These delineators – what the early white performers in black face called themselves – acquired many of their ideas and material from slaves in the south. The slaves were seen entertaining themselves, or their masters, at fairs, Church functions, dances and holidays. One dance in particular was called the 'Juba', which was always celebrated on New Year's Day, accompanied by hand clapping, banjo, violin and rattling bones. It later became one of the most popular dances within the delineators' programmes.

Whenever we examine slavery in America, most of us link this foul institution mainly with the Southern region, but there was also the act

1. Victorian Christmas card c.1890s

2. Ashtray or card stand, Painted wood, 35 inches high, British, c.1930s

3. Three-dimensional Victorian christmas card, c.1890s

4. Party name cards, c.1900s

5. Die-cut minstrels, c.1900s

1. *Produce label, USA, 1940s*

2. *Chad Valley toy banjo with black figures, Metal, 18 inches high, 1940s*

3. *Oxo advertising die-cut 'Oxo for Children', c.1910*

4. *Die-cut figure, British, c.1890s-1900s*

5. *USA patent for doll designed by Katherine T Donovan, 1924*

of subjugation in the North. By 1800 the practice was on the decline, as black labour was unimportant to the economy in the North as well as in Great Britain and in Europe. English anti-slavery campaigners, headed by William Wilberforce, gained their first major conquest in 1801 when Britain did away with, banned, and made illegal, all business and trade in African slaves by British citizens. Slavery was finally abolished by Act of Parliament in 1833, thirty years before President Lincoln issued the Emancipation Proclamation, both acts allegedly freeing slaves.

It is no coincidence that compassionate opposition to the practice of slavery began among urban and industrialized populations who, because of the tremendous efficiency of alternative steam power, could well afford to begin to despise slavery. In most instances, there are geographic, rather than ethical reasons why the 'compassionate' opposition to slavery began in England, northern Europe and northern America. All of these regions had industrial economies suited to the introduction of steam power. In such areas agriculture became less important economically. Tropical regions in contrast had to rely extensively on manual labour to harvest the plantations which were the basis of their economy. Mobile steam power with sufficient power for industrial production only came later.

President Lincoln announced the Emancipation Proclamation only after the Confiscation and Military Acts of 1862 had made emancipation irreversible, and when he needed black manpower to fill the ranks of the Union Army. At the same time, the whites could seem democratic, while the contribution of black people to their own emancipation was down played.

Although, blacks could purchase their freedom, they could not vote, and with the influx of so many Europeans, work was unavailable. Therefore blacks lived in poverty and isolation, with little or no interaction between themselves and whites. Becoming mostly invisible and of little concern to the white community, attitudes, opinions, influences, and stereotypes about blacks were not as strong as in the South.

In such a social climate in the North, the music halls and theatres had a change of atmosphere. Where, at one time only the so-called upper classes attended, a wider cross-section of the community became theatre-goers. These 'new' audiences did not only sit and watch, but participated with the performers. It was in this environment that the delineators' shows thrived. Possible the most popular delineator of that period was Thomas D Rice, who had seen slaves in the south singing and dancing.

Rice's shows were a great success, and soon many other performers travelled the South in search of material for the eager audiences in the North. Often, a few delineators would unite and create a larger pageant, which led to what is now referred to as the Minstrel Show.

Probably the first of these was presented in New York in February 1843. Four black faced delineators presented a production of 'oddities, peculiarities, eccentricities and comicalities, of the sable genus of Humanity' (Robert C Toll, *Blacking Up: the Minstrel Show in Nineteenth Century America*). They cast aside the term delineators, and called themselves *The Virginia Minstrels*. After a huge success, the American public were shouting for more, resulting in the formation of other groups in virtually every big city of the North. Many travelled west and south, but most performed in the north-east. Another troupe called *The Ethiopian Serenaders*, were one of the first socially accepted minstrel troupes in America, appearing at the White House in Washington DC around 1844. They later went abroad to London, and after a conquering London, launching at the Hanover Square Concert Rooms in 1846, they appeared at numerous other venues, making it possible for all subsequent minstrel troupes to perform in Europe. They disbanded in 1900.

The minstrel's acclaim is attributed to the need for American entertainment and an interest in black culture by Northerners, British

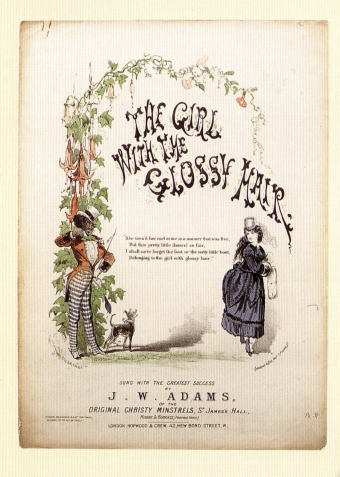

Above: Die-cut, fold-out paper minstrel show by Birn Bros, London, c.1880s-1890s

Left: Sheet music (British) 'The Girl with Glossy Hair', c.1890

Below: Christmas sticker, c.1940s

and Europeans. Many of these people believed they were seeing authentic black performers, rather than whites in blacked up faces.

The minstrel performers exploited the distinctiveness of blacks inside the plantation community, strengthening fixed perceptions of racial inequality. Minstrels created a type that ignored the actual details of the lives many African-Americans conducted as self-sufficient individuals. Instead, they provided an image in opposition to the reality much of the public experienced in urban and rural societies. Minstrels degraded blacks to a demeaning status, with the distorted physical appearances and foolish behaviour typical of the acclaimed founders like Daniel Emmet and TD Rice. Minstrelsy became so far removed from its origin in the black slave culture, that it failed to depict real life.

As the popularity of the Minstrel Show grew in America, Britain and Europe began to welcome many travelling troupes. The acclaim was overwhelming, especially in Britain, and minstrels began to form troupes there. The *Moore and Burgess Minstrels* were one such

Die-cut figures of minstrels,
British, c.1890s

troupe, assembled by the American George Washington, 'Pony' Moore (an avid equestrian), and business manager, Frederick Burgess.

Another group called the *Mathews Brothers Christys Coloured Comedians* played at the Polygraphic Hall in November 1864. They used the title made famous in America by the original *Christy Minstrels* (created by EP Christy in 1846). The *Christy Minstrels* visited London in 1857.

Many of the racially stereotyped images of black people, which have thrived in western culture for the past 170 years have been fuelled by the black faced minstrels.

It is important to note that during the minstrel period, some troupes had mixed casts – black performers who would 'black-up' with burnt cork just as the white actors did. They also had to produce buffoonish, degrading and grotesque characters. One of the most popular black performers in minstrelsy was William Henry Lane who was credited with the popularity of the 'Juba' dance. Born a freeman in Providence, Rhode Island, he later began working with some of the best performers, and soon gained top billing as 'Mr Juba'. Later known as the 'king' of dancers, he died at the young age of twenty-nine in London, in 1852.

Another popular black performer and composer was James Bland. This black American was born in 1854 and studied law at Howard University in Washington DC. To earn extra money he learned to play the banjo and performed in various hotels. After meeting many ex-slaves, who worked on the campus, he became interested in their type of music. Soon after, he left his studies to become a minstrel in several all-black troupes like, Billy Kersans, *Callender's Coloured Minstrels*, and *Spraque's Georgia Minstrels*. In 1881 he went to Europe and performed without burnt cork. He wrote over 600 songs for himself and other minstrel performers, many of whom published his work as their own. By 1900 the interest in minstrels was waning in America and upon his return to the States, he found little or no work and died in poverty in 1911. His many songs include; *Carry me Back to Old Virginny* and *Oh, Dem Golden Slippers*.

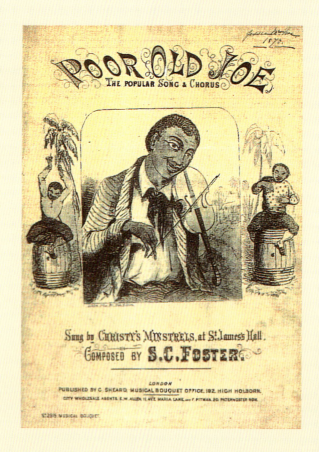

Left: Sheet music of song 'Poor Old Joe', British, 1872

Below left: Christmas card by Raphael Tuck & Sons, c.1900s

Bottom left: Liebig tea card, c.1900

Below: Chrismas card, one of three designs by F Langbridge, c.1880s-1890s

Bottom: Greetings card, British, c.1890s

Right: Page from a book, Title unknown, British, c.1900s

Far right: Paper cut-out, c.1900s

Below: Greetings card, British, 'HMS Black Tar', c.1900s

Bottom: Confectionery cards, Chocolat Gilbert, c.1900s

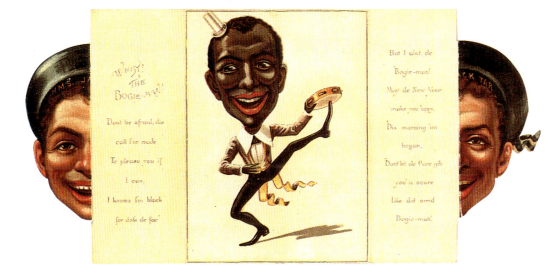

Black performers had to 'black-up' even though they disapproved of the practice. Images often show a smiling face with a lot of teeth. In line with the tendency towards caricature – the smile was painted on in all of the popular shows. This painted smile gave the impression of constant joy and politeness, regardless of any provocation which might arise – always the 'cheerful slave' who was dehumanized and abused every waking hour. Thus minstrels were seen as mindless robots who would respond like string puppets and continuously smile even when struck or made to endure back-breaking servitude.

Why did blacks help to perpetuate this degradation by joining these minstrel troupes? I believe for a number of reasons. Firstly, blacks had no position in society on which they could rely, and minstrelsy was an escape from more degrading and backbreaking work. It was often a choice between joining these troupes or possibly starving. Many had to support other members of their family who could not find work of any kind in the industrial north. Working in a minstrel troupe not only gave them gainful employment but notability as well. With this fame, black performers received what was actually 'pseudo' social acceptance.

Secondly, some blacks observed white performers imitating black culture and felt they could produce a more exciting portrayal. Even if it was to be excessive, it was after all, 'stolen from us'.

Thirdly, many blacks with the gift of performing were eager to express their talent and after years of social and economical prohibition, any opportunity that presented itself was acceptable, no matter how degrading.

Unfortunately, some of these negative images still exist in western culture in literary, artistic and social attitudes. To a certain extent, blacks cannot free themselves from their minstrel past.

Minstrels & gollies featured in sheet music

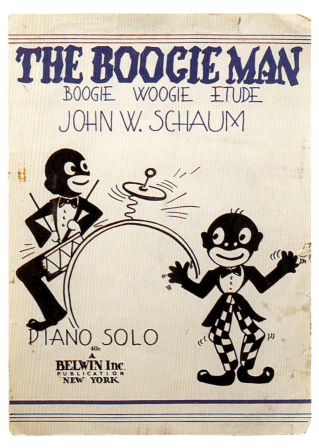

Sheet music

I Don't Think I'll Say Anymore

British, 1910

Sheet music

The Boogie Man

USA, 1944

Sheet music

Ten Little Nigger Tunes

Ten songs, British, 1928

Sheet music

Babau!

British, 1920s

Opposite:

Sheet music

The Golliwog. Two-step

Illust: Sidney Kent

British, 1909

Sheet music

Whistling Rufus

British, 1899

Sheet music

Niggardly Nigger

British, late 1800s

Sheet music

It Aint Gonna Rain No Mo'

British, 1923

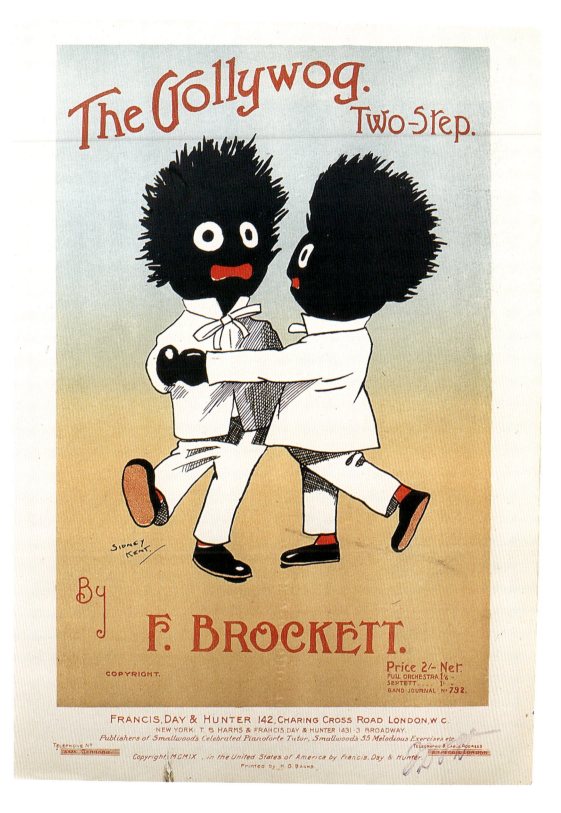

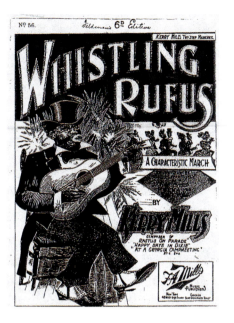

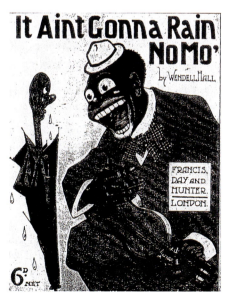

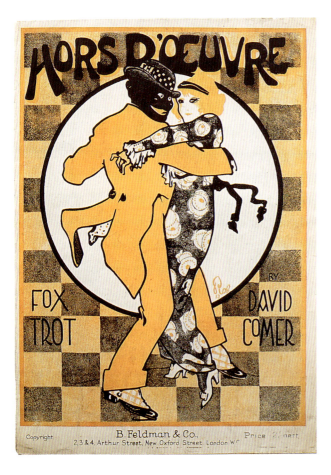

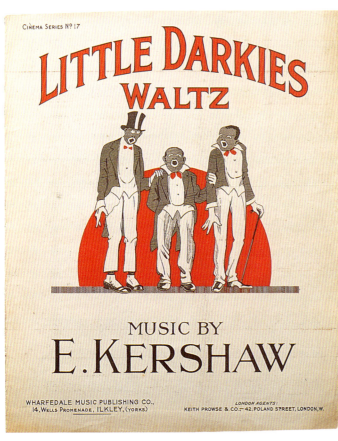

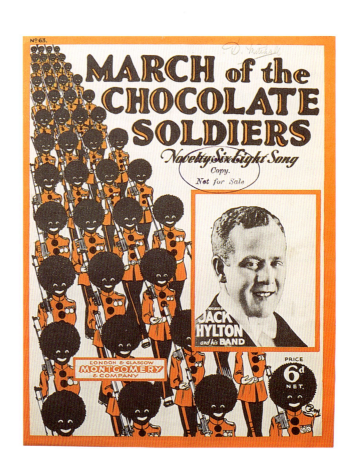

Sheet music

Hors D'Oeuvre

British, 1919

Susannah's Squeaking Shoes

British, 1923

Little Darkies Waltz

British, c.1900

March of the Chocolate Soldiers

British, 1929

Opposite:

Golly Eyes

British, 1922

By the same composer as the successful fox trots 'JICKY' and 'WEDDING TIME.'

Price 2/- net.

"Golly Eyes"

One Step by Lee Rudd

ASCHERBERG HOPWOOD & CREW Ltd. 16 Mortimer St. W.1.
(FOR COLONIAL & FOREIGN AGENTS SEE BACK PAGE.)
PRINTED IN ENGLAND BY LOWE & BRYDONE PRINTERS LTD., LONDON. N.W.10.

Florence Upton & the Golliwogg

Items of nursery china based on the 'Golliwogg' books

The original Golliwogg with the Dutch Dolls, Sarah Jane (left) and Peggy Deutchland (right), on loan to the Museum of Childhood, Bethnal Green. Photograph courtesy of the V&A.

Child's cup, saucer & dish, 'Ivoryware Hancocks', handpainted, English 1923-37

Child's cream jug, German, c.1905

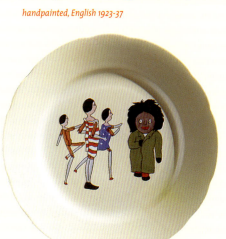

Child's china dish, German, c.1906

Child's china tea bell, German, c.1906

Child's green egg and teapot, German, possibly 'Heubach' or 'Rudolstadt', c.1905

Child's toy sugar jar, German, (lid missing), c.1905

On 22 February 1873, Florence Upton was born in Flushing, Long Island, New York to an English emigré couple, Bertha and Thomas Upton. After a comfortable early childhood in an artistic environment, the elder girls and their mother, found themselves supporting the family following the sudden and premature death of their father. Florence, the eldest daughter, had to leave school, and chose to become an illustrator, while her mother, Bertha, who was a talented singer, gave voice lessons. This successful arrangement enabled them to save up enough money to travel to England to meet other members of their family.

Having been in England for several years, Florence obtained a commission in 1894 to contribute her first series of illustrations for a book entitled *Pax and Carlino* by Ernst Beckman – a story of a boy who is kidnapped, escapes and befriends a dog. While searching for his mother, he meets a negro on board a ship to America and is eventually reunited with his family.

Illustrating someone else's story, gave Florence the confidence to create her own children's book, using dolls that she had in her possession. A number of jointed wooden dolls called Dutch Dolls and a rag minstrel doll with a shock of real fur black hair, round black leather face and white shell button eyes and stitched with black cotton thread, caught her attention. The body of the golliwogg was made of heavy black muslin, he was cotton filled and definitely hand made.

Florence completed *The Adventures of Two Dutch Dolls* for publication in 1895, the first of a series of thirteen books featuring *The Golliwogg*. Florence drew the pictures, while her mother wrote the verses.

Initially, there were problems in finding a publisher for the book, but soon Mr Allen of Longmans, Green & Co. in London agreed to publish after seeing his children enjoying the twenty-two year old Florence Upton's drawings. Although the book was a success, some parents were concerned that their children would be frightened by *The Golliwogg*. On the contrary, he became the most popular of all the characters and remained so throughout the series.

However, the family failed to copyright their creation and so *The Golliwogg* image was exploited in the same way as Helen Bannerman's popular *Little Black Sambo* had been treated. Even so, the success of the book enabled Florence to pursue her art training in Europe.

In the stories *The Golliwogg* was considered to be the 'Prince of Golliwoggs', a brave, lovable and intelligent, yet mischievous gentleman. He

led the Dutch dolls into many adventures around the world, meeting new and exciting people, places and situations. Their journeys were often fraught with danger, but *The Golliwogg* always managed to overcome all obstacles, while protecting the dolls.

The thirteen books in the series were reprinted many times until the late 1970s.

During World War I, Florence put her original manuscripts and toys up for auction in aid of the Red Cross. A sum of £472.50 was raised, which covered the cost of an ambulance called *The Golliwogg*, which was destined to go to the front line of battle. The buyer of the items presented them to the Prime Minister and they resided at Chequers, in Kent, the Prime Minister's country home, until they were recently moved to the Museum of Childhood, Bethnal Green in London.

Left: 1895. The Adventures of Two Dutch Dolls.
The popularity of the Golliwogg was such that the publisher ensured that all future books would contain 'The Golliwogg' in the title

Below: Postcard published by Raphael Tuck & Sons, 1903

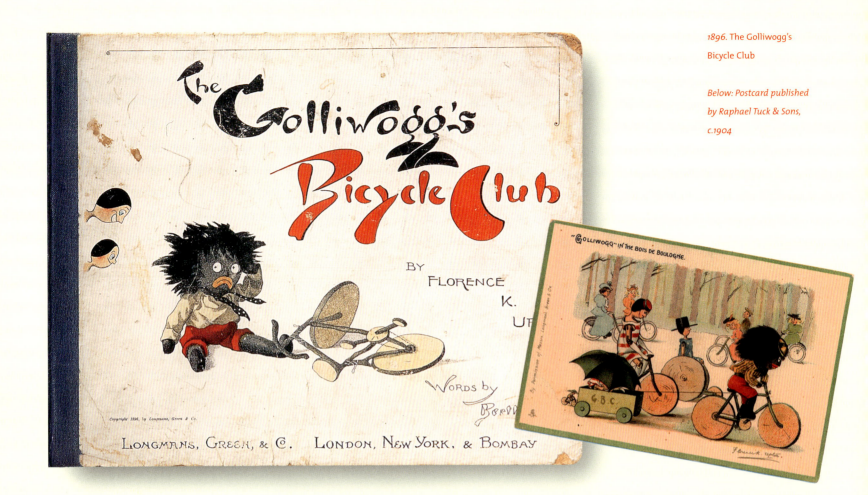

1896. The Golliwogg's Bicycle Club

Below: Postcard published by Raphael Tuck & Sons, c.1904

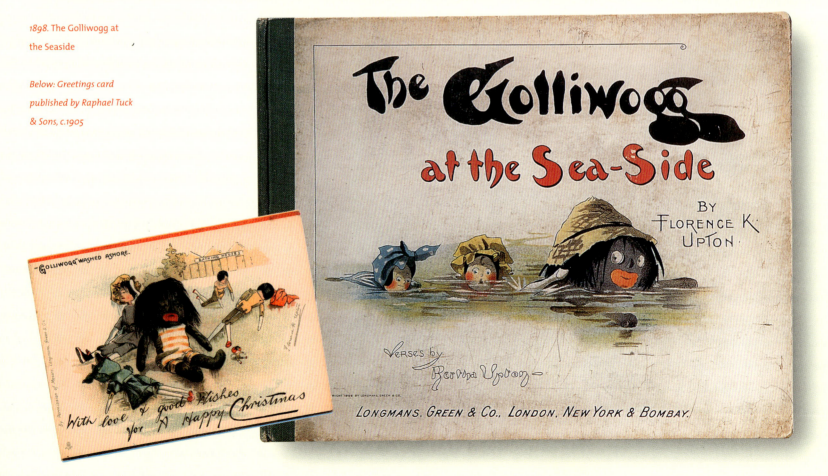

1898. The Golliwogg at the Seaside

Below: Greetings card published by Raphael Tuck & Sons, c.1905

1899. The Golliwogg in War!

Below: Postcard published by Raphael Tuck & Sons, c.1905

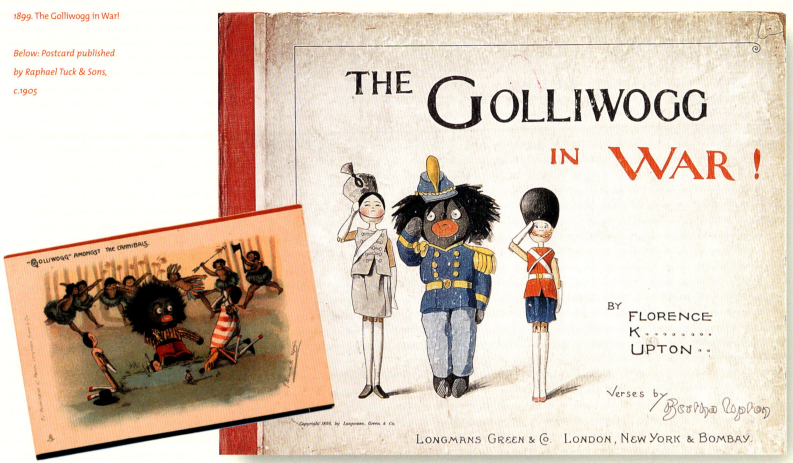

1900 The Golliwogg's Polar Adventures

Below: Postcard published by Raphael Tuck & Sons, c.1905

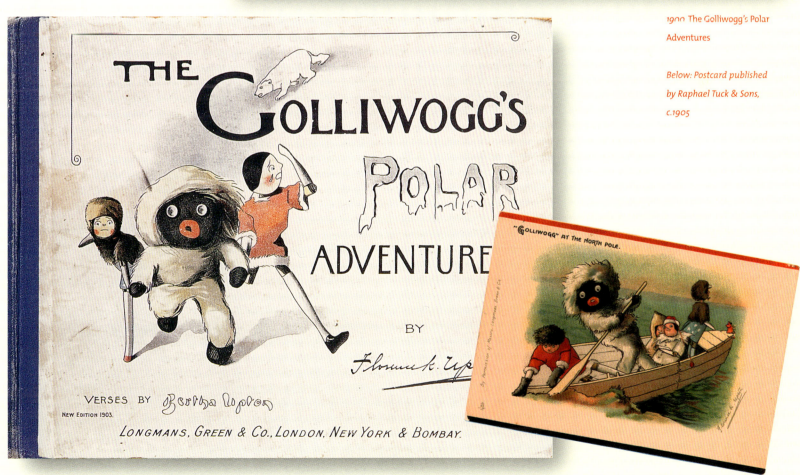

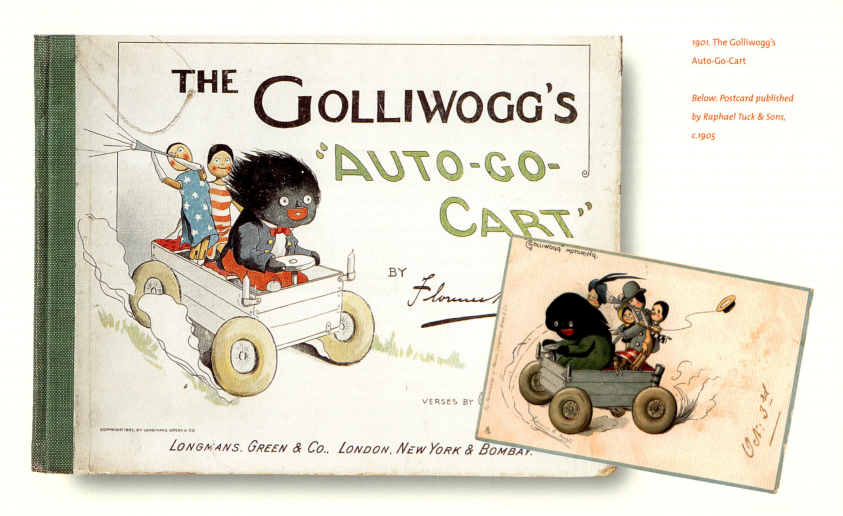

1901. The Golliwogg's
Auto-Go-Cart

Below: Postcard published
by Raphael Tuck & Sons,
c.1905

1902. The Golliwogg's
Airship

Below: Postcard published
by Raphael Tuck & Sons,
c.1906

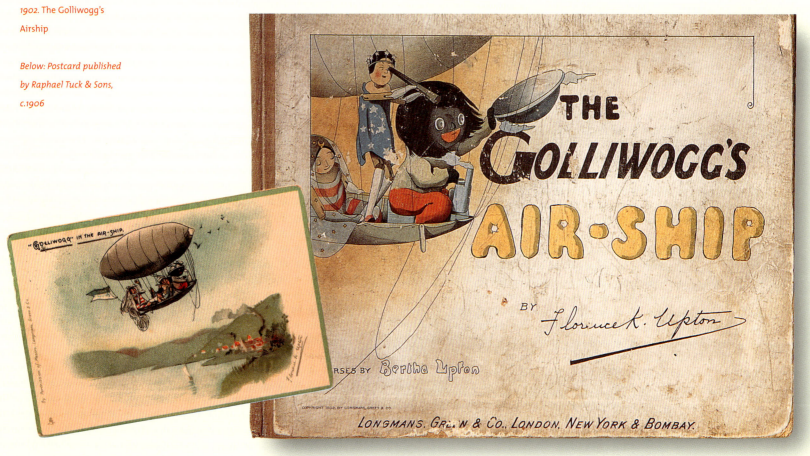

1903. The Golliwogg's Circus

Throughout the series, we still find the Golliwogg to be a charming creature. It is no wonder children loved this gnome. In each book he takes the dolls on a new adventure, this time to the circus!

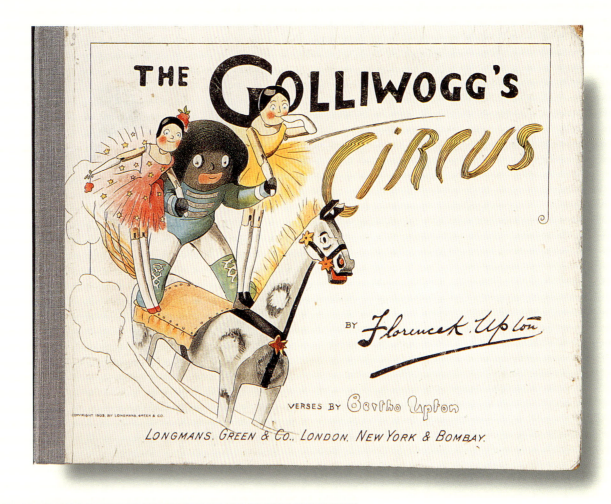

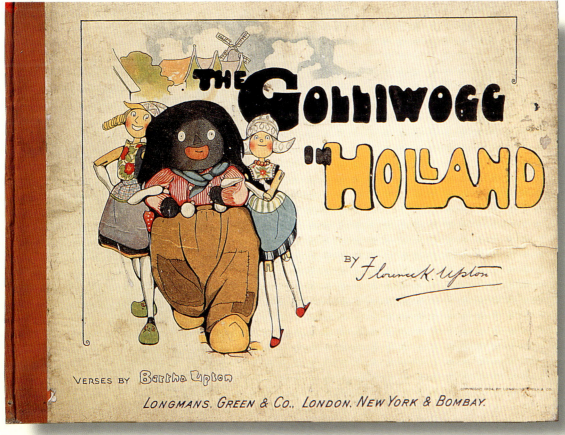

1904. The Golliwogg in Holland

The Golliwogg not only takes the Dutch Dolls to Holland, but he also showers them with gifts. He seems to know so much about the world. To children he is a magician

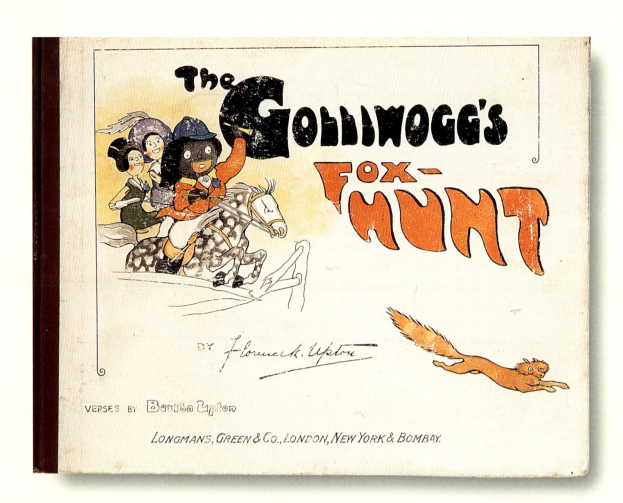

1905. The Golliwogg's
Fox-Hunt

The Golliwogg is sometimes
referred to as a 'dog ', but
it becomes apparent that
he is adventurous,
inventive, endearing,
trustworthy and brave,
but he can also be clumsy,
naughty and reckless

The Golliwogg takes the
dolls on a fox hunt where
again trouble strikes, but
all ends well

1906. The Golliwogg's
Desert Island

In this story the Golliwogg
and the dolls travel to a
desert island, where they
meet a tribesman

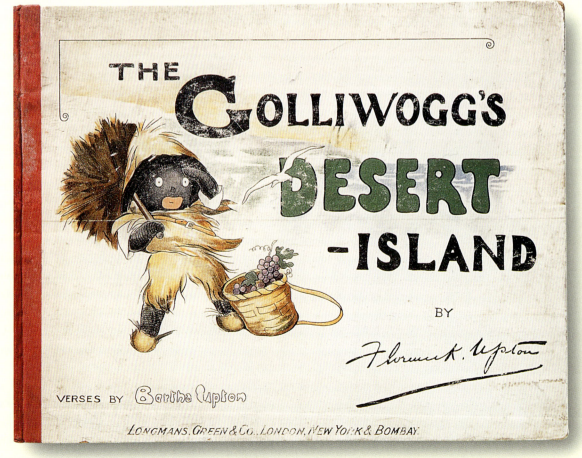

1907. The Golliwogg's Christmas

The Golliwogg plans a great Christmas for the dolls, but in his clumsiness all goes wrong. In the end the dolls express their appreciation and love for him and they all have a Merry Christmas

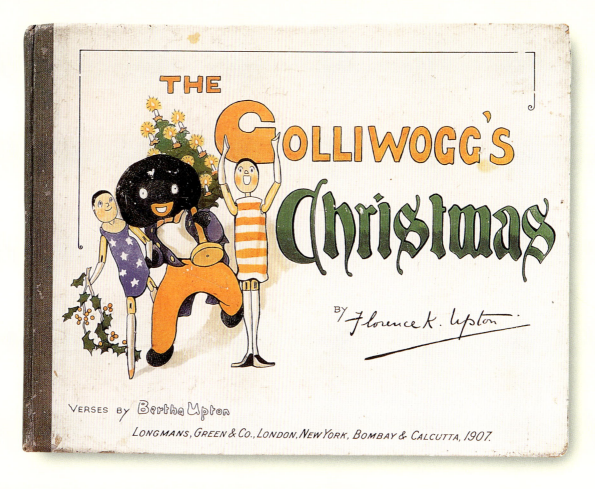

1909. The Golliwogg in the African Jungle

The stories and adventures end with the near killing of the Golliwogg at the hands of African natives until the dolls plead for his life

Sambos & golliwogs in children's books

Sambos & golliwogs in children's books

On this and the following pages, you will get an idea of the extent of mass-produced children's books and ephemera which include images of Black people and golliwogs, published between the mid-19th century and the mid-20th century. However, due to their popularity (among white children), we can show only a few, as the total output was colossal.

Ten Little Nigger Boys seemed to be one of the most popular perennial favourites down the years, so we have devoted two double page spreads to a range of examples.

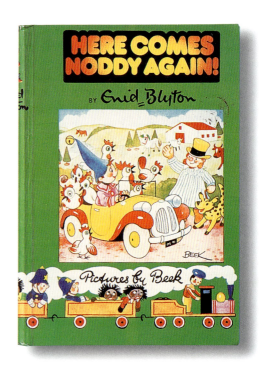

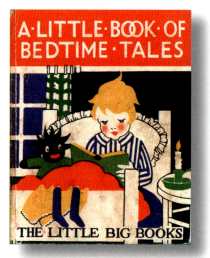

Far left: Piccaninny ABC
Pub: Dean's Rag Book Company
1905

Above left: Toy Book, Pub: Anon,
c.1920

Left: A Valentine's Toy Book
Pub: Valentines, 1913

Top: Here Comes Noddy Again
Pub: Anon, nd

Above: A Little Book of Bedtime Tales
Illust: May Smith
Pub: Humphrey Milford, 1929

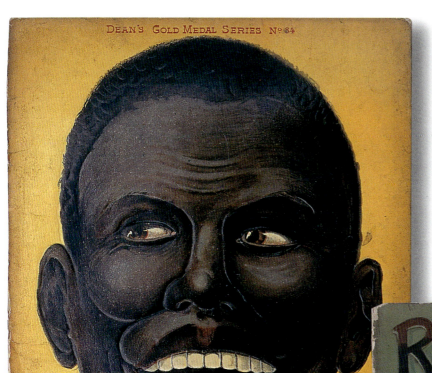

Left: The Darkies' ABC
Illust: Vernon Barrett
Dean's Gold Medal Series
Pub: Dean & Son, c.1901

Below: Riddle-Me-Riddle-Me-Ree
Illust: Vernon Barrett
Dean's Gold Medal Series
Pub: Dean & Son, c.1901

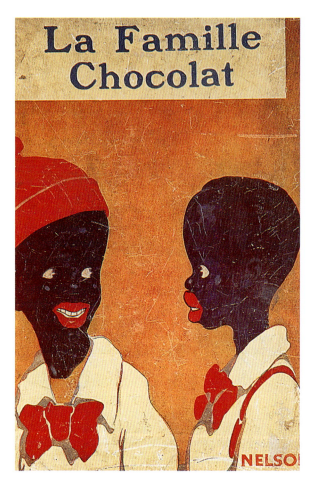

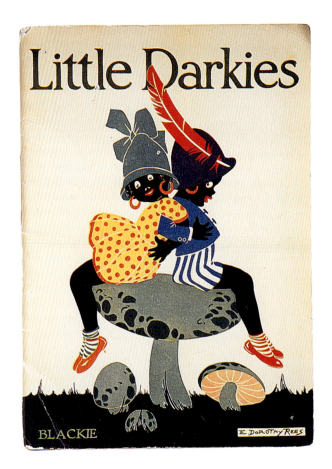

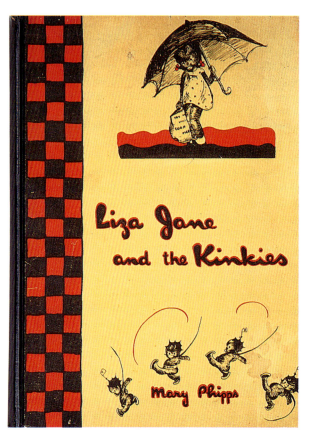

Far left: The Babes in the Wood
A Tom Thumb Picture Book
Pub: Anon, 1908

Left: Little Darkies,
Pub: Blackie & Son, c.1920s

Below left: La Famille Chocolat
Pub: Nelson, c.1930

Below: Liza Jane & the Kinkies
Author & illust: Mary Phipps
Pub: JH Sears & Co, New York 1929

Opposite:
Left: Round de Ole Plantation,
!llust: GF Christie
Pub: Blackie & Sons, c.1900

Right: Sally & Sambo go Travelling
Pub: Raphael Tuck & Sons c.1940s

Below left: Tiny Tots' ABC, *c.1940s*

Below right: Dinah Jum & Mac,
Pub: Anon, c.1940s

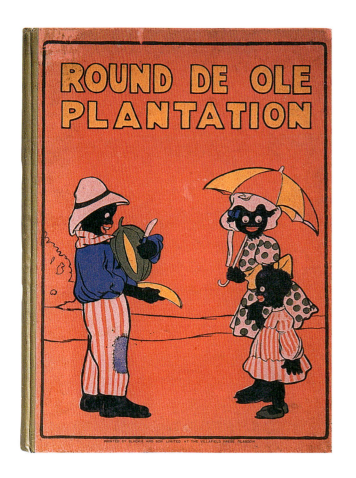

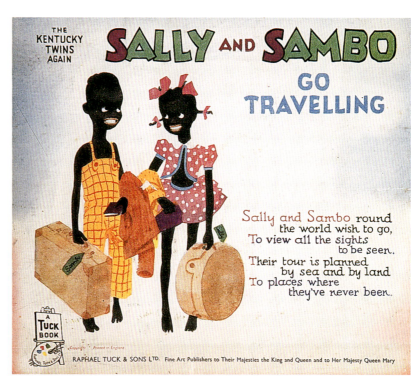

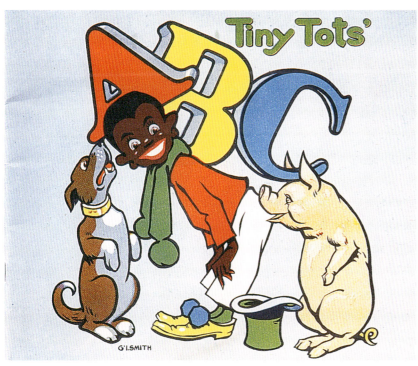

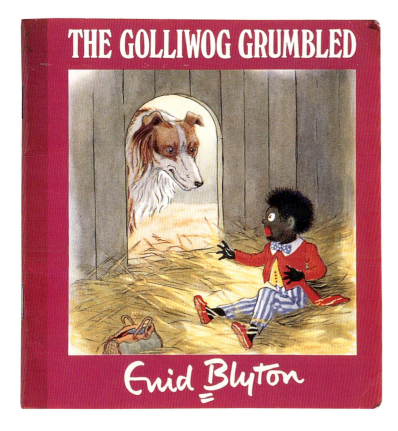

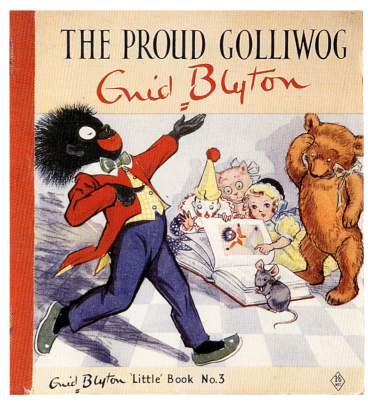

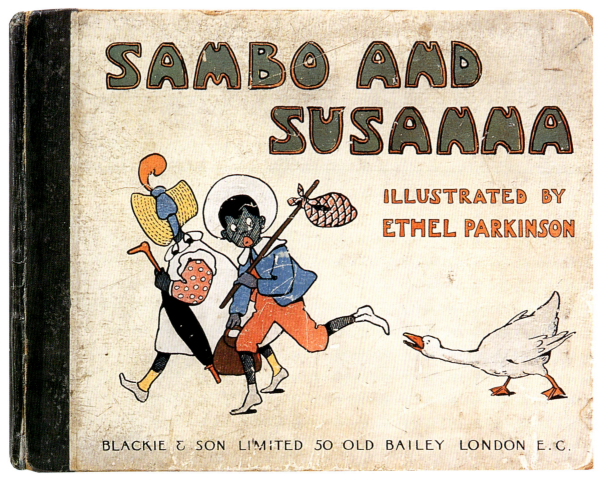

Above left: The Golliwog Grumbled
Author: Enid Blyton
Pub: Anon, c.1950

Above: The Proud Golliwog
Author: Enid Blyton
Pub: Anon, c.1950

Left: Sambo & Susanna
Illust: Ethel Parkinson
Verses: May Byron
Pub: Blackie & Son, c.1909

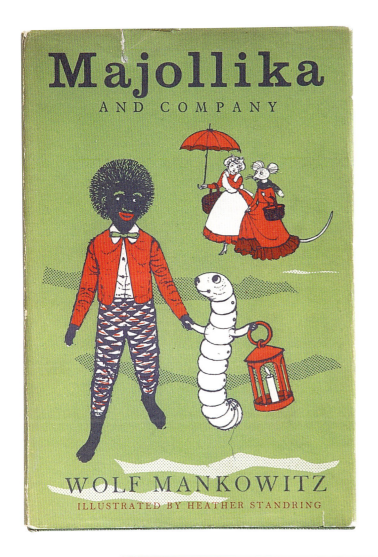

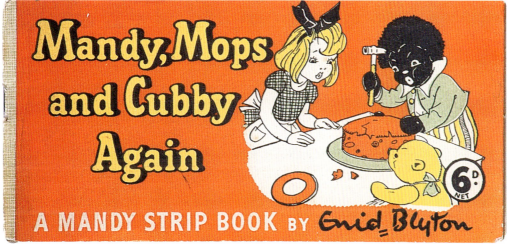

Above left: Majolica and Company
Author: Wolf Mankowitz
Illust: Heather Standring
Pub: André Deutsch, 1955

Above: Eb' and Flo' Annual
Pub: Dean & Son, c.1940s

Left: Mandy, Mops and Cubby Again
A Mandy Strip Book
Author: Enid Blyton
Pub: Anon, c.1950s

Above: Fairyland Tales
Uncle Jim's Pantomime
Pub: Anon, 1927

Above right: The Runaway Toys
Pub: Anon, c.1930s

Right: Freddy Frizzylocks
Illust: Angusine MacGregor
Verses: Olive Clark
Pub: Blackie & Son, 1914

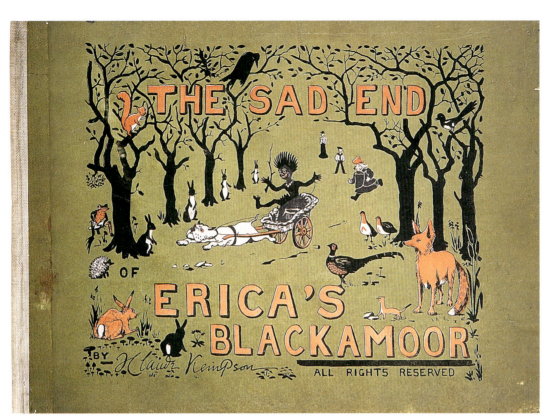

Left: The Sad End of Erica's Blackamoor
Author: Claude Kempson
Pub: Anon, 1903

Below left: The So Long Book of Golliwog Tales
Illust: Justin Michman
(Artist's rough and printed book)
Pub: Anon, 1940s-1950s

Below: Golly Tales
Tall Book Series
Pub: Anon, 1940s-1950s

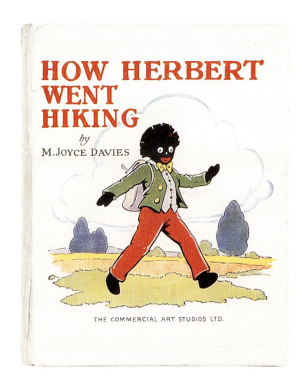

Above: Golly 'I Squeak'
Pub: Anon, c.1940s

Above middle: Teddy and Sambo
Picture and Story book
Pub: Anon, c.1940s

Above right: How Herbert went
Hiking
*Pub: Commercial Art Studios
c.1950*

Right: Bobo's Adventures
Pub: Anon, c.1915

Far right: Bobo's by the Sea
Pub: Anon, c.1915

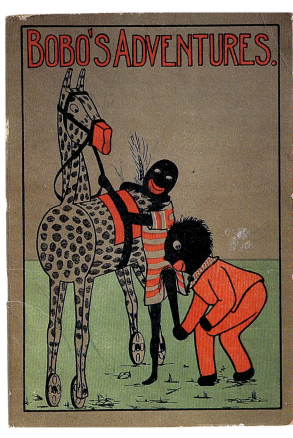

Right: The Toy Town Tiger

Author & illust: Ernest Aris

Pub: Anon, c.1917

Far right: More Sabo Stories

Author: EW Lewis

Pub: Hodder & Stoughton, 1926

Below: The Teddy Bear Book

Illust: Albert Earnest Kennedy

Pub: Collins, 1938

Below right: Sunshine Corner

Pictures and Story Book

Pub: Anon, c.1940s

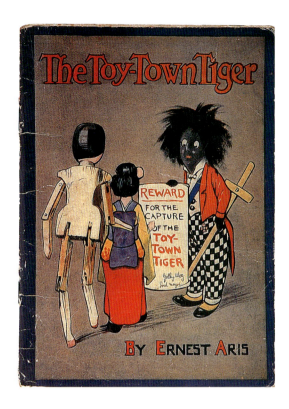

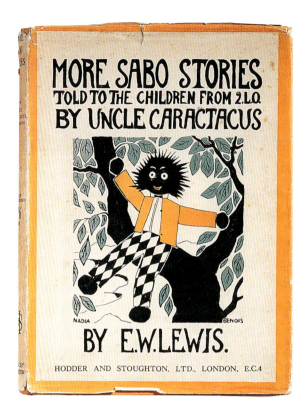

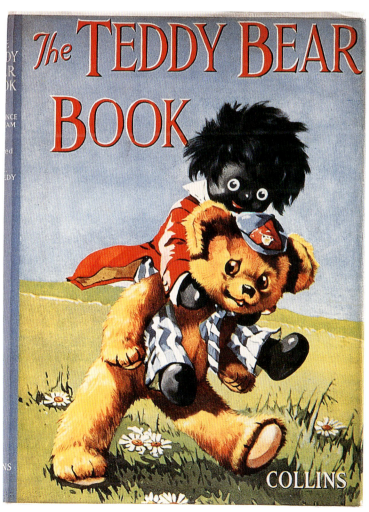

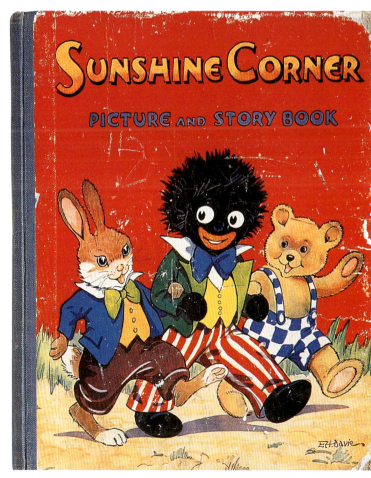

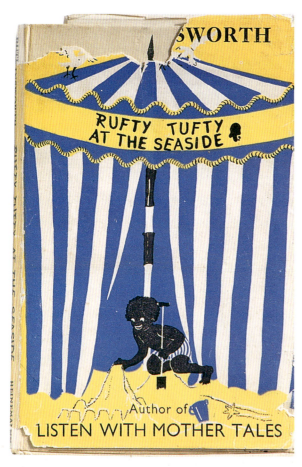

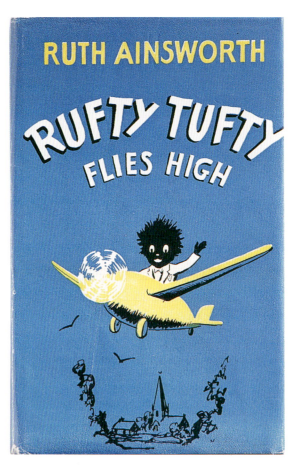

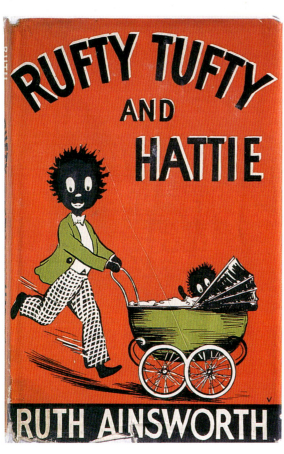

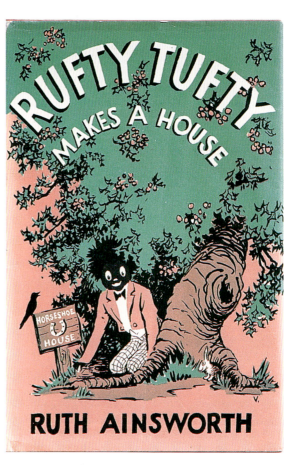

Far left: Rufty Tufty at the Seaside
Author: Ruth Ainsworth
Pub: Anon 1954

Left: Rufty Tufty Flies High
Author: Ruth Ainsworth
Pub: Anon, 1959

Below left: Rufty Tufty and Hattie
Author: Ruth Ainsworth
Pub: Anon, 1962

Below right: Rufty Tufty
Makes a House
Author: Ruth Ainsworth
Pub: Anon, 1965

Right: The Story of Little
Black Sambo
Author: Helen Bannerman
Pub: Anon, 1930s

Far right: Epaminondas Helps
in the Garden
Author: Constance Egan
Illust: Albert Earnest Kennedy
Pub: Anon, 1959

Below: My Bedtime Book
Pub: Anon c.1940s

Below right: Jolly Golly's
Painting Book
Pub: Anon, c.1950s

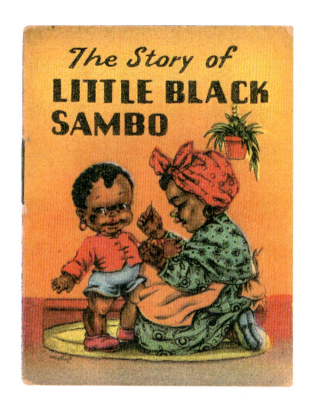

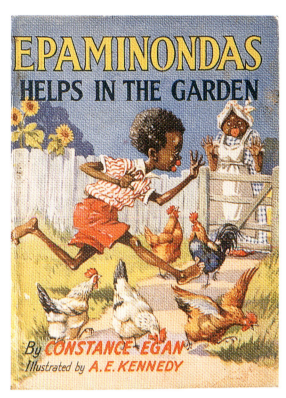

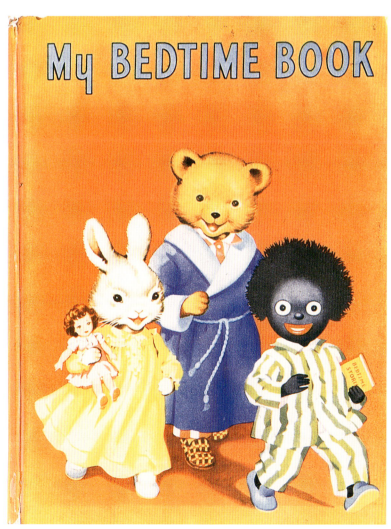

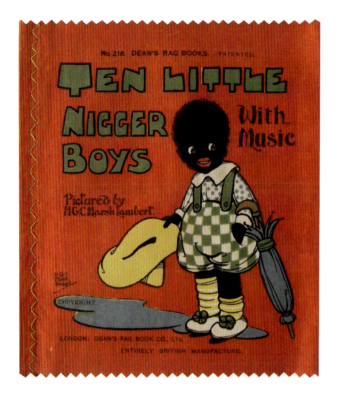

Far left: Ten Little Nigger *Boys*

Illust: HGC Marsh Lambert

Pub: Dean's Rag Book Co, 1918

Left: Ten Little Nigger Boys,

Pub: Garratt's Stores, c.1930s

Below left: Ten Little Niggers,

Dean's Pinafore Series,

Pub: Dean & Son, c.1890s

Below: Ten Little Negroes

Pub: Anon, 1945

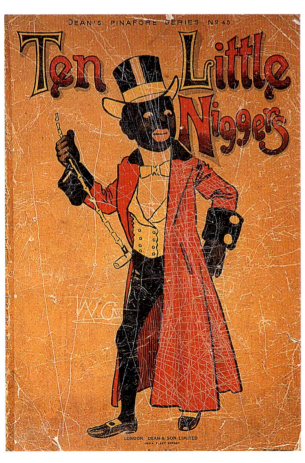

Below: Ten Little Nigger Boys

Valentine's Toy Books Series

Pub: Valentine's, 1914

Right: Ten Little Niggers

Pub: Anon, c.1910

Below right: Ten Little Nigger Boys

Father Tuck's Nursery Series

Pub: Raphael Tuck & Sons c.1920

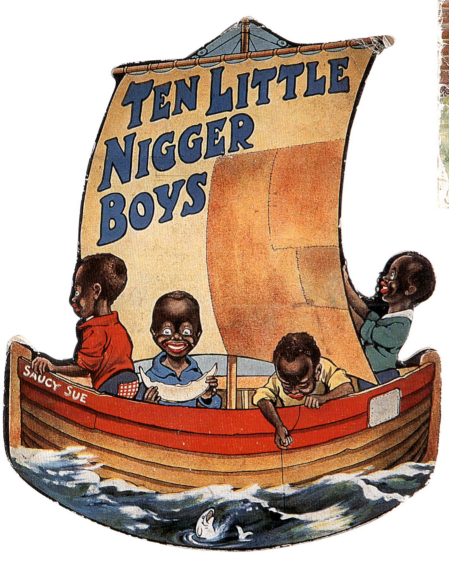

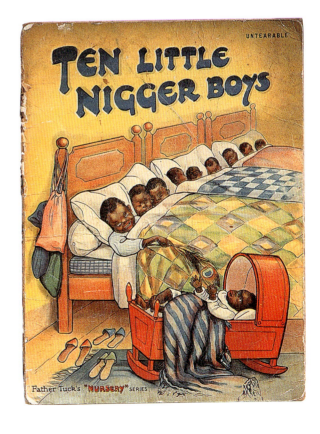

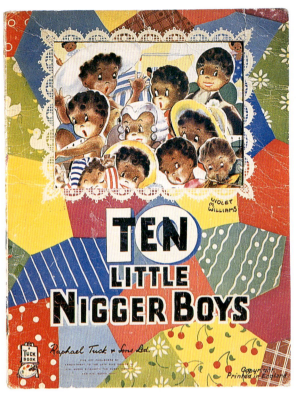

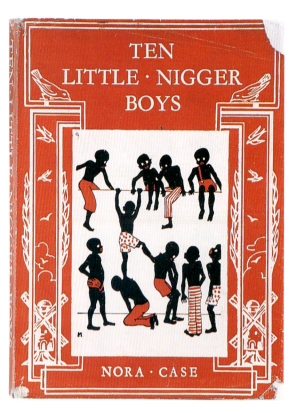

Far left: Ten Little Nigger Boys,
*Pub: Raphael Tuck & Sons,
c.1940s*

Left: Ten Little Nigger Boys,
Editor: Nora Case, c.1957

Below left: Ten Little Nigger Boys,
Pub: Nelson, c.1930s

Below: Ten Little Nigger Boys,
Pub: Anon, c.1940s

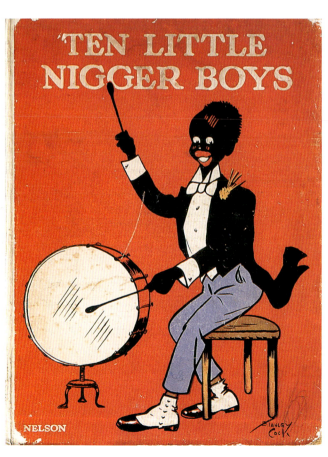

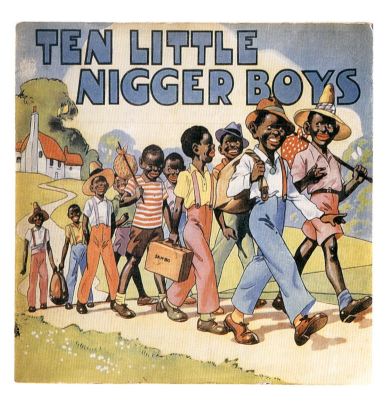

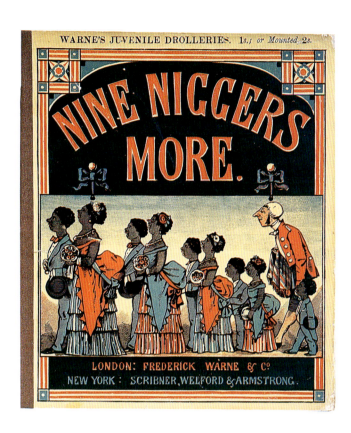

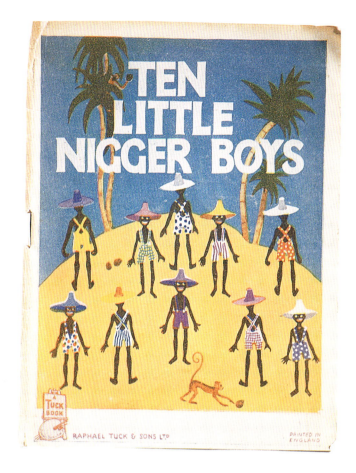

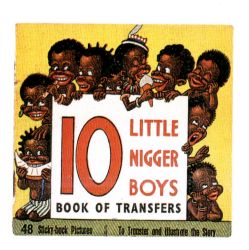

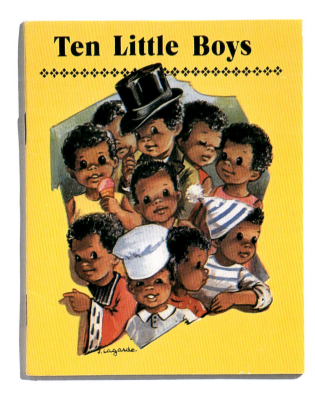

Above left: Nine Niggers More
Pub: London: Frederick Warne
New York: Scribner, Welford &
Armstrong, c.1890s

Above: Ten Little Nigger Boys
Pub: Raphael Tuck & Sons
c.1940s-1950s

Middle left: Ten Little Nigger Boys
Pub: Tuff Books, c.1940s

Far left: Ten Little Nigger Boys
Book of paper transfers
Pub: Anon, British, 1908

Left: Ten Little Nigger Boys,
Pub: Brown & Watson
c.1960s

More black characters in children's literature

Black characters are often portrayed in children's literature as either mischievous, villainous or grotesque, but here are two books that are part of a trilogy, the first being entitled *The Golliwog News*. All three feature John James as the main character in the adventures. He is intelligent and brave and is the editor of a newspaper, *The Golliwog News*. Atkinson Ward (an English newspaper editor) and his wife wrote the stories under the pseudonyms Philip and Fay Inchfawn. Illustrations for the *Treasure* volume were by FC Ward and *Diamond* was illustrated by Thomas Maybank. The publisher was SW Partridge.

Grotesque images illustrated by AE Kennedy in Constance Egan's Epaminondas, *c.1950s*

THE COURT OF THE FLOWERS

wogs were clustering about him just as though he too were a king.

"Yes, here he is," cried Golly. "This is Tony. Tony, here are my brothers—Mumbo, Jumbo, Lumbo, and Dumbo. Dumbo can't talk, you know."

Golly's brothers were so like Golly himself

that, in that first meeting, Tony did not know one from the other, but he told himself that there were sure to be things to distinguish them by.

"Do you know, Tony," said Mumbo, "we are so glad you have come. The dwarfs and elves of Golliwog have declared war on the fairies, and, of course, we shall fight with the fairies against the dwarfs and the elves, and

11

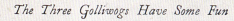

The Three Golliwogs Have Some Fun

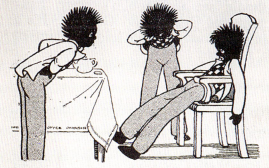

"Where's the paper?" asked Woggie.

open, marched into the parlour and fell into a chair, panting. The other two golliwogs looked at him.

"Where's the paper?" asked Woggie.

"Surely you haven't been all the way there and back and come home without the paper after all!" said Nigger.

"I'll tell you what's happened," said Golly, and he told the story of the goblin and the dog. "And you

103

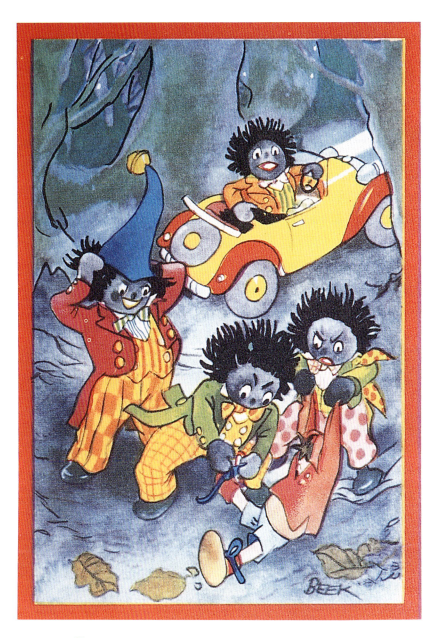

Here Comes Noddy Again – In the Dark, Dark Wood, *the book that sparked controversy. Notice how the black characters mug the innocent looking white character, 1960s*

Above left: From Draycott M Dell's Golliwog Island, *1934*

Left: From The Three Golliwogs *by Enid Blyton. 1940s*

Golliwogs in postcards & greetings cards

1. *Postcard, British,*
Illust: GE Shepheard, 1906

2. *Postcard, British, c.1920*
Illust: FG Lewin

3. *Postcard, British, c.1903*
'You are my honeysuckle,
I am the bee'

4. *Bamforth postcard, British,*
Taylor Tots, 1960s

5. *Postcard, British,*
Illust: D Tempest, 1930s

6. *Postcard, British, c.1921*

7. *Postcard, British, c.1910*

8. *Greetings card, British, c.1890*

9. *Silk postcard, British, 1907*
based on the Upton dolls

10. *Postcard, British, c.1903*

11. *Greetings card, British, c.1930*

12. *Postcard, British, c.1910*

13. *Postcard, British, c.1905*

14. *Postcard, British,*
Illust: Sydney Carter, c.1905

15. *Postcard, British, c.1909*

16. *Postcard, British, 1910*

17. *Postcard, British,*
Illust: FG Lewin, 1923

1

2

3

6

7

8

12

13

14

4

BLACK LOOKS NEVER GOT ANYBODY ANYWHERE.
LET'S BRIGHTEN YOU UP A BIT!

5

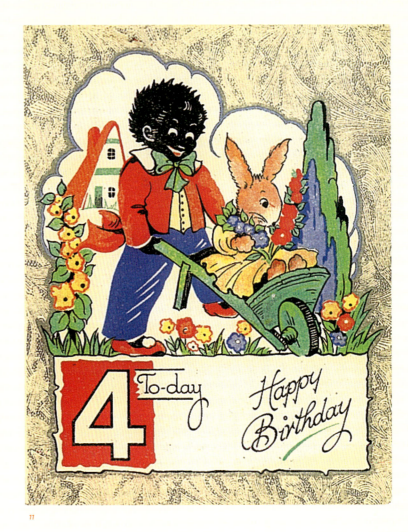

11

9

10

"HE'S BITING!"

15

16

Bobbed!

17

1

2

6

7

11

12

16

17

18

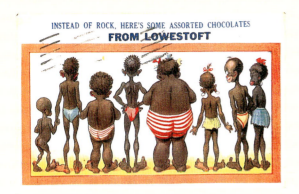

INSTEAD OF ROCK, HERE'S SOME ASSORTED CHOCOLATES
FROM LOWESTOFT

3

4

With Best Wishes for a Happy Bithday

5

Women and children first, Rastus !

8

"Nigger: 'fore we married youse said you'd lay down your life for me, Now youse wont even lay down de carpet !"

9

With every good wish

10

God made the little niggers, He made them in the night,
He made them in a hurry, and forgot to make them white.

13

HAPPY BIRTHDAY TO YOU with lots of FUN too. From

14

THE DOLLIES' TEA PARTY

15

OUR GREETING ON YOUR BIRTHDAY

We've just come by the post, to say
We're Mr and Mrs Golly;
We hear it is your Birthday,
We hope it will be jolly.

19

May the New Year meet you with a smiling face.

20

21

A Christmas Be Yours Midst Music and Song. Sweet Voices Surround You All Day Long.

"HARK I HEAR THE ANGELS SING."

22

1. Modern postcard, British

2. Postcard, British, c.1900

3. Christmas card, British
Pub: Newton Mill, c.1947

4. Birthday card, British, c.1940s

5. Hand drawn postcard, 1904

6. Modern postcard, British, c.1980s

7. Postcard, British, c.1910

8. Postcard, British, c.1900

9. Christmas card, British, c.1947

10. Postcard of Miss Ethel Oliver
Pub: J Beagles & Co, c.1905

11. Postcard, British, c.1920

12. Birthday card with black fairies,
British, c.1930

13. Christmas postcard, British,
Pub: Valentines c.1910

14. Postcard, British, 1923

15. Bithday card, British, c.1930

16. Postcards, framed set showing
various activities, British c.1920s

17. 'Cut-out' postcard, British
Illust: William Henry Ellam
Pub: WE Mack, c.1920

18. 'Cut-out' postcard, British,
Pub: WE Mack, c.1920
Toy Town Series

19. Postcard, British
Illust: Agnes Richardson
Pub: Millar & Lang, 1924

20. Postcard, British
Illust: Linda Edgerton
Pub: J Salmon, 1935

1

2

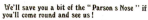

6

7

11

We'll save you a bit of the " Parson s Nose " if
you'll come round and see us !

12

13

16

3

4

5

8

9

10

14

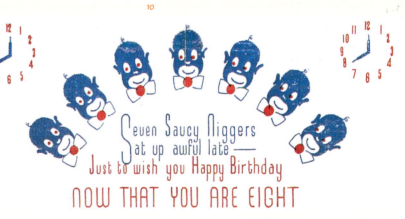

15

17

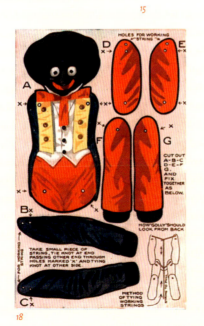

18

19

20

Golliwogs in toys, games & nursery china

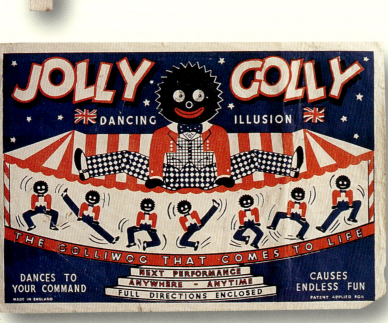

1. Creamer featuring characters from 'Noddy', British, c.1960s

2. Egg-cup & spoon set, British, c.1910

3. Paper puppet, British, c.1920s

4. Puzzle game, British, c.1940s

5. Pot-metal bank by John Harper c.1925. Made in cast iron, pot metal & brass. Beware of reproductions, especially brass series, 1920s-1960s

6. Package containing a dancing golliwog, British, c.1940s

7. Wind-up tin toy, possibly French, c.1950s

8. Happynack, Seaside Pail Co, British, c.1950s

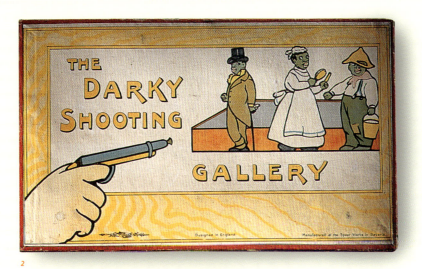

1. Tom Tom Jungle Boy
7 inches high, Japanese, c.1950s

2. Children's game. Note the cruel
method of disposing of black
people, British, c.1905

3. Dancing toy, British, c.1940s

4. Golly ball game, by Dodo
3 x 3½ inches, British, 1980s

5. Jack-in-a-box mug, British, 1960s

6. Tin bank, British, c.1960s

7. Bisque figures, gnome & golly
jack-in-a-box, c.1920s.
(Sally Letham collection)

Golliwog ashtray stands

1. Ashtray stand,
painted wood, c.1930s

2. Ashtray stand, painted
wood, 32$\frac{1}{2}$ inches high,
c.1930s

3. Ashtray stand, painted
wood, 36 inches high, c.1940s

4. Twin golliwogs, ashtray or
card stand, painted wood,
37 inches high, c.1920s

'GOLDEN SHRED'
THE FAMILY FAVOURITE

Robertsons advertising, 1980s

Opposite:
1. The Club Plantation,
advertisement, St Louis, 1940s

2. Mansell's celluloid
indicarors, 1920s-1930s

3. Gartex rubber golly
advertisement, 1955

4. Darkie toothpaste, known
throughout the Far East for
the minstrel log on the tube.
The name was changed to
Darlie in Taiwan & Hong Kong
after American civil rights
activists required the trade
mark to be removed. The logo
continued for a while until it
was eventually banned

Advertising featuring the minstrel
& the golliwog

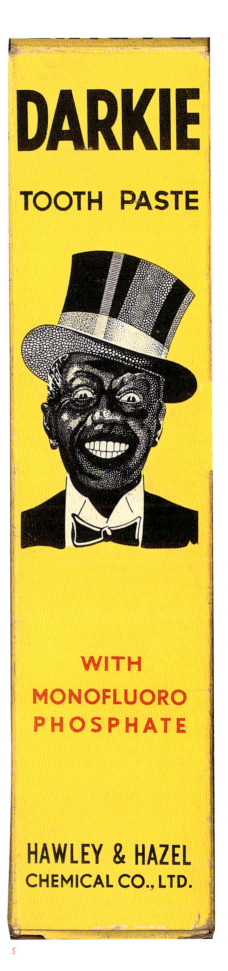

Child's nursery rug, featuring golliwog, gnomes & elves, British, c.1930

Child's nursery rug, All Aboard 33 x 22 inches, Worth & Co, c.1930

1. Letter opener, painted wood,
6 inches high, c.1930s

2. Jack-in-the-box, British, c.1930

3. String holder, British, 1940s

4. Yoruba mask, Nigeria, c.1920s

5. Hantel pewter golly pendant,
1½ inches high, 1980s

Sambos & black people in journals and magazines

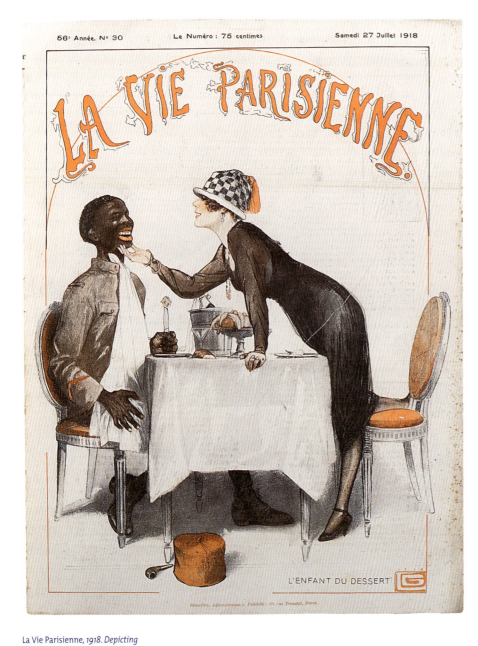

La Vie Parisienne, 1918. Depicting
a black man's appetite for white
women was not uncommon

Right: Magazine page 1920s. Note
how the black man fondles the
white woman

Opposite: Life magazine cover
1926

From a French magazine, 1919.
Notice how grotesque the black
man looks

Life

JULY 15, 1926   PRICE 15 CENTS

L. J. Holton

Every thing is Hot-tentotsy now

The manufactured golliwog

The main criterion of manufactured golliwogs is the quality control which is part of the production process, a factor seldom found in the home made or cheaply made doll. This does not mean that factory produced dolls are always more interesting or durable, but they were carefully conceived and assembled by trained designers and operatives. They were tested to meet specific regulations and safety standards, which quite often assured durability. Many companies had a marketing department which examined the extent of the doll's appeal for adults and children alike. The most durable fabrics and accessories were used, and generally the dolls were hygienically safe. Therefore, the amount of extra care taken by responsible companies results in toys which command higher prices in the collector's market.

　　Buy the best examples you can find of the dolls you desire. If the doll is in poor condition, but scarce or early, acquire it, as it may be some time before you find another in better condition.

Unknown manufactured golliwog, similar to the Fondle golliwogs of the same period. Stuffed with cotton, 10 inches high, c.1930s/1940s

Synthetic wig
Painted features
Buckram face
Ribbon bow-tie
Cotton shirt, hands, trousers and feet

French 'Bairritz' dolls,
three of four musicians.
(The dealer who sold me the
dolls called them 'golliwogs'),
c.1920s-1940s

Manufactured golliwog with chime, located in chest. Felt & sailcloth, stuffed with kapok, 19 inches high, maker unknown, c.1950s-1960s

Synthetic pile wig
Joggle eyes
Felt face & mouth
Ribbon bow tie
Sailcloth waistcoat, jacket, trousers, hands and feet
Plastic buttons

Far right: Golliwog similar to the Dean's golliwog of the 1930s
Imported into the USA by Lenart Imports Ltd.
kapok filled, stuffed with wood wool, voice box located in chest, maker unknown, c.1930s-early 1940s.
Unlikely to be a Dean's golliwog, as the eyes are not joggle or plastic, as used by the company during the 1930s. Neither did Dean's golliwogs have voice boxes, suggesting this high quality doll was made by one of the other leading manufacturers

Mohair wig
Linen face & hands
Linen-backed shoe-button eyes
Felt mouth
Bow tie (missing)
Felt jacket
Velveteen waistcoat & trousers
Cotton feet

Some of the finest golliwog dolls were created by firms such as Atlas, Allwin, Chad Valley, Dean's, JK Farnell, Givjoy, Merrythought, Omega, Wendy Boston and others. At one time or another some of these companies employed the same designers or managers; however, each golliwog was unique.

Manufactured golliwogs at times are easier to identify and date even without their labels. But you must explore the information available in books and at museums, fairs, dealers, etc. After a short period, you will begin to become more knowledgeable about these items.

Golliwog similar to Dean's,
but overall shape suggests not,
possibly Merton, kapok filled,
19 inches high, c.1950s

Robertson's golliwog,
Stuffed with cotton similar to
the later Chad Valley dolls,
12 inches high, c.1960s-1970s

Synthetic pile wig
Felt eyes & mouth
Sailcloth face
Felt mouth
Ribbon bow tie
Sailcloth clothing

Mohair wig
Linen & felt eyes
Felt face & mouth
Ribbon bow tie (missing)
Felt jacket & waistcoat trousers
Jacket buttons (incorrect)
Felt hands
Cotton feet

At times you will find the clothing, hair or facial features have deteriorated or been altered by age and 'improvements'. I strongly advise you never to try to restore or improve any part of a doll unless you can match the original materials and pattern with an identical replacement, (which very few people can do). You risk altering the original design which reduces the value of the doll. For example, it is quite difficult to achieve the symmetrical die-cut features and clothing as on the manufacturer's original. This also applies to printed, processed or painted features. Duplicating the materials, colours, textures and styles can be very complicated, even if you have knowledge of the original design. Unless you employ a professional restorer, you should leave the doll as you find it.

Scarce golliwog with a green face & pink hair. Looks like a punk character or an alien. British maker unknown, c.1960s

Hand puppet golliwog British maker unknown, c.1970s

Synthetic pile wig
Felt eyes & mouth
Cotton body

Cheaply-made golliwog.
Plastic eyes & buttons
c.1970s

Manufactured golliwog
All felt, cotton filled.
c.1970s

All cotton golliwog
Plastic eyes & nose
All felt, cotton filled.
Maker unknown.
c.1980s

Wendy Boston Toys

In 1940, due to the bombing of Birmingham, a British couple, Ken and Wendy found themselves homeless. Ken was invalided out of the RAF, so his job as a wartime journalist was over. Wendy also lost her job as a commercial artist. After moving to the country, their costs began to mount and Ken took on a series of odd jobs, interrupted by spells in hospital. Wendy began making soft toys from odds and ends, with the idea of giving them away as Christmas presents. So, while Ken was convalescing, Wendy was building a business. Many retail stores began to order her toys and the Wendy Boston Soft Toys Company got underway, Boston being Wendy's maiden name.

By 1945, her shop in Wales had a staff of three – Wendy, Ken and a girl. Two years later it had grown to sixteen. The factories, at Queen Street Abergavenny, Monmouthshire and Castle Road, Crickhowell, Breacon (opened in 1948), employed thirty members of staff. This was the year that the firm invented the safe lock-in eyes. It was around this time they produced their first golliwog, cunningly created in one piece and not jointed. This doll could sit and loll wherever it was put. At about 18 inches high, it was made of a heavy cotton, stuffed with straw. All features except the nose and jacket were printed on the cloth. The trousers and waistcoat were red, with white bow tie attached, and the blue jacket sported yellow lapels and two brass buttons. The nose was the famous lock-in black button while the other facial features were printed. This golliwog's entire body was brown in colour while later versions came in black.

Golliwog
Wood-wool stuffed
14 inches high
c.1940

Short cotton pile wig
Printed features
Lock-in button nose
Rayon ribbon bow tie
Felt jacket
Cotton pile body
Brass buttons
Printed waistcoat & trousers

Golliwog
Foam stuffed
18 inches high
c.1950

Golliwog
Foam-filled
18 inches high, c.1950

Synthetic wig
Sailcloth face & body
Printed features
Ribbon bow tie
Corduroy jacket
Plastic buttons
Mitten-type hands

Synthetic wig
Printed features
Plastic buttons
Sailcloth face, body & skirt,
Corduroy jacket & shoes

Golliwog, 1958

Scottywog, 1954

Golliwog
13 inches high
Foam-filled, c.1950

Synthetic wig
Printed features
Sailcloth body

Golliwog
Foam-filled
14 inches high
c.1950s

Golliwog
Foam-filled
18 inches high
1950s

Short cotton pile wig
Printed features
Sailcloth face & body

Synthetic wig
Printed features
Sailcloth face & body
Ribbon bow tie
Corduroy jacket
Plastic buttons
Flat mitten-type fingers

Chad Valley Toy Co.

The Chad Valley Toy Company, established in 1823 as a book binder and printer, was based in Lichfield Street, Birmingham and was owned by Anthony B Johnson. In 1860, after moving to George Street, Birmingham, the business added stationery printing to its various operations. The company took the name Chad Valley after moving to Harbourne near Birmingham in 1897. A factory was built along the Chad stream and in 1919 the trading name, Chad Valley, was registered. Over the years, an array of boxed games were launched, still under the Johnson family's management.

Woolly Wag, kapok stuffed
12 inches high, c.1920
Other sizes: 14 & 18 inches

Mohair wig
Linen-covered card
Lock-in type eyes
Painted mouth & nose
Felt collar & satin bow tie
Linen buttons
Jointed arms & legs
Velvet body & jacket

Woolly Wag
Kapok stuffed
18 inches high
1920s to 1930s

Mohair wig
Linen painted eyes
Painted mouth & nose
Felt collar & satin bow tie
Velvet body & jacket
Linen buttons
Jointed arms & legs

Chad Valley took on an additional factory in 1915 at the old Harbourne Institute and later, a building in Wellington, Shropshire, committed to producing dolls and soft toys. Other factories were incorporated by Chad Valley, who, by then, made promotional toys. During the early 1920s the firm produced many soft dolls and bears and during the late 1920s they introduced their first golliwogs, including golliwogs on tricycles. Stuffed with kapok, they wore the same colours as the jointed versions and were about 12 inches high. These trike golliwogs were also softer, which enabled the attached feet to spin on the turning pedals when pulled. The jacket was made of velvet but the rest of the doll was of a silky fabric. Chad Valley continued making the jointed version until the early 1940's.

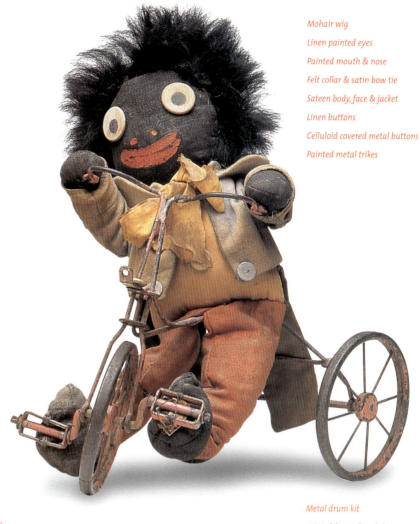

Mohair wig

Linen painted eyes

Painted mouth & nose

Felt collar & satin bow tie

Sateen body, face & jacket

Linen buttons

Celluloid covered metal buttons

Painted metal trikes

Woolly Wags on tricycles
(caresse dolls) kapok stuffed
12 inches high, c.1920s

Metal drum kit
printed four colour litho
1940s

Woolly Wag

Silky-cotton

Kapok stuffed

(missing jacket and tie)

13 inches high, 1920s

Long pile wig

Painted linen eyes

Painted nose

Painted mouth

Toy bank, c.1940

Woolly Wag

Kapok stuffed

11 inches high

1920s to 1930s

Long pile wig

Painted linen eyes

Painted mouth & nose

Felt collar & satin bow tie

Velvet body & clothing

Linen buttons

Jointed arms & legs

The silk plush golliwogs, which also varied in size, were almost identical to the Merrythought doll of the same period, and unless there is a label, you can easily be confused.

In 1947, when production had nearly ended, only a limited assortment of velvet type dolls were still on hand. After 1948 the company turned to making cheaper dolls and soft toys. All doll production ended in 1957. The golliwog continued to be produced as a soft toy and these soft dolls of the early 1950s are hard to find. Even locating any of the 1950s catalogues is a difficult task so there is little available on record.

In 1931 Chad Valley bought out Peacock and Company Ltd of London, then in 1938 received a Royal Warrant of appointment as 'Toymakers to her Majesty the Queen'. During the Second World War the company cut game and toy production severely to make clothing for children at Wrekin Works. Then in 1946 the company manufactured an assortment of rubber dolls and toys after the purchase of Waterloo Works, Wellington. The company continued to acquire other toy manufacturers during the 1950s and Chad Valley itself became a public company in 1950. By 1960 the companies Holland and Lane Limited, Robert Bros. Limited and Acme Stopper and Box Company Limited had been absorbed by Chad Valley.

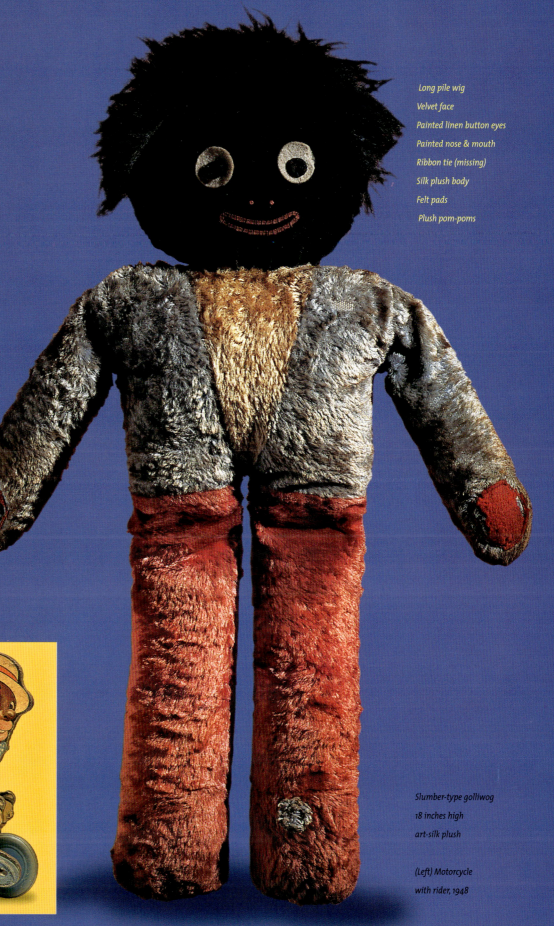

Long pile wig
Velvet face
Painted linen button eyes
Painted nose & mouth
Ribbon tie (missing)
Silk plush body
Felt pads
Plush pom-poms

Slumber-type golliwog
18 inches high
art-silk plush

(Left) Motorcycle
with rider, 1948

Golliwog
12 to 16 inches high
Cotton filled, 1966

Short pile wig
Painted features
Sailcloth face & body
Rayon bow tie
Felt jacket
Felt buttons

Advertisement for a
Chad Valley golliwog, 1955

Possible Chad Valley golliwog
10 inches high
Cotton filled
Bought at Woolworth's
Late 1960s–early 1970s

Short pile wig
Painted canvas eyes
Painted nose & mouth
Flannelette torso
Sailcloth arms and legs

Golliwog
20 inches high, 1960s

Long pile wig
Felt eyes & nose
Ultrasuede mouth
Cotton collar
Rayon bow tie
Sailcloth jacket,
waistcoat & trousers
Felt buttons

In 1955, one of the Chad Valley golliwogs had a blue jacket made of a cotton sailcloth fabric, a yellow waistcoat with two black felt buttons, red trousers, a green and white polka dot bow tie and a white collar. The face had felt eyes and nose with a red artificial suede mouth and white painted cotton fabric for teeth. This golliwog looked very much like the Chad Valley dolls of the late 1950s and early 60s.

The 1960s golliwogs are easier to find. They are basically the same as the 1950s versions, the difference being that the 1960s version had trousers striped in red, yellow, black and blue. They also had blue felt eyes and two red felt dots for the nose. As in the earlier version the clothing was not removable. The sizes ranged from about 32 inches to 12 inches.

During the mid-1960s Chad Valley began to print the facial features not unlike Dean's. The golliwogs of this period began to resemble the American Raggedy Andy dolls. As with the 1950s and eary 1960s dolls, they had black synthetic wigs. Although the materials used during this period were of cheaper quality, the dolls still had character.

In the 1970s all but two factories closed and by 1978 Palitoy had taken over. The golliwogs produced during this time were so cheaply made that they are hardly worth a mention. The best examples produced in the 1970s were by Merrythought, Pedigree, Burbank and Dennis. Golliwogs were also out of favour during these years due to the fact that children wanted more sophisticated toys and dolls. Chad Valley golliwogs were made in a similar style to Dean's dolls but lacked the quality. Some golliwogs were cheaply produced in Spain which are almost identical to the Chad Valley doll, looking very much like a rag doll with red lapels, blue jacket, red and white striped trousers, printed white circles for eyes and a red mouth. These golliwogs lack character and quality. Chad Valley ceased production in the early 1980s and Woolworth's bought the tradename Chad Valley in 1988.

Golliwog
16 inches high
Cotton filled, 1966

Short pile wig
Painted features
Sailcloth face, body & jacket
Rayon bow-tie
Felt buttons

Short pile wig
Lock-in eyes / felt backing
Lock-in plastic nose
Felt mouth & buttons
Rayon bow-tie
Sailcloth body

Chad Valley-Chiltern golliwog
10 inches high
Cotton filled
Made after the takeover of
Chiltern Toys in 1968

Golliwog
11-20 inches high
Foam filled
1950s to 1960s
These golliwogs came in
different fabric combinations

Plush wig, face, upper body
& hands
Felt-backed plastic eyes
Plastic nose & buttons
Felt mouth
Ribbon tie (missing)

Golliwog
34 inches high
Foam filled
1950s to 1960s

Synthetic wig
Sailcloth face
Printed eyes &
mouth
Cotton shirt
Fabric buttons
Sailcloth jacket
Cotton hands
Sailcloth legs
Cotton feet

Dean's Rag Book Co.

Dean's Rag Book Company was founded in 1903, as an associate company of the famous publisher, Dean & Son. Its innovative idea, conceived by Henry S Dean, the managing director, was to produce indestructible childrens' books from unbleached calico cloth. The first book, printed in 1902 was hand blocked, in two colours, folded and tied with silk ribbon. It sold for six shillings.

All subsequent rag books until World War II were printed in up to eight colours by the litho process using copper rollers. They were exported around the world. Their success steered the company into producing printed dolls on sheets of cloth, for children to cut out and make up themselves. For those unable to make the dolls, the company sold them ready-made. Dean's Rag, Knockabout Toy Sheets, 'Washable and Hygienic' were patented in 1908. Like the rag books, they carried the trademark of an English terrier and bulldog having a tug-of-war over a rag book, along with the slogan claiming, *Wear Ever – Tear Never*. Dean's wide range of cut-out doll sheets, including black dolls, were popular up to World War I, and although they continued well into the 1920s ready-made 'character dolls' gradually took their place.

In 1923 Dean's introduced its first golliwog doll. Although not called a golliwog it most clearly was one. *Wooly Wally* as it was called, was described as brightly dressed, strongly made, 'the wild wig is like the tame smile, it

'Evripoze' Golliwog
18 inches high
Cotton filled, 1966

Synthetic pile wig
Plastic lock-in eyes
Felt mouth
Ribbon bow-tie (missing)
5 button type (two missing)

(Below left)
Dancing Darkies:
Uncle Remus
Massa Bones
Massa Johnson

(Below) Wooly Wally

'Evripoze' golliwog
18 inches high
Cotton filled, 1966

Synthetic pile wig
Plastic lock-in eyes
Felt face
Lace collar & cuffs
Felt jacket, skirt & shoes

Dean's Dancing Dolls

won't come off'. The reference number was D 284. Dean's produced *Wooly Wally* until around 1928. During this time the doll was offered riding a folding scooter which added one inch to its height of eleven inches. At that time Dean's introduced *Dancing Dolls* – pairs of brightly dressed 14½ inch dolls. The series included golliwog dolls, one of which had white hair. Made from felt like the *True to Life* styled dolls, they also had joggle eyes, and were available together or separately.

In 1935 Dean's offered their 'new' golliwog to the public. It was made of brightly coloured felt with non-removable clothing, eight buttons (four on the jacket, four on the waistcoat) joggle eyes, felt mouth and mohair wig. This golliwog came in three sizes: 10 inches (D832); 14 inches (D833) and 18 inches (D835). Stuffed with kapok for hygienic purposes, it remained in production into the early 1940s. Along with *Wooly Wally*, all Dean's golliwogs and other black dolls dating from the 1920s to the early 1940s are rare. In the late 1940s through the early 1950s the company produced another felt golliwog (number D424, 18 inches). Brightly

Golliwog

Dean's ref: D424

1940s

Evripose golliwog

Dean's ref: D405

1940s

Synthetic wig

Linen button eyes

(should be plastic joggle eyes)

Felt face & mouth

Synthetic pile wig

Joggle eyes

Felt face & mouth

Felt bow tie

Golliwog

Dean's ref: D424

Opened fingered version

20 inches high

1940s

Synthetic pile wig

Joggle eyes

Felt face & mouth

Felt bow tie

Felt body

10 button type

Evripose golliwogs
Dean's ref: A405
1950s
There were size & colour
variations (see below)

Mohair wig
Joggle eyes
Felt face, mouth & body
Ribbon bow tie (not original)
5 button type

Synthetic pile wig
Plastic lock-in eyes
Felt face & mouth
Ribbon bow tie (not original)
Felt body
5 button type

Synthetic wig

Plastic lock-in eyes

Felt face & mouth

Ribbon bow tie (not original)

5 button type (3 missing)

dressed with ten buttons (six on the jacket, four on the waistcoat), the face was almost round (as in numbers D832/ 835). With rolling disc eyes, wool or mohair wig and stuffed with kapok, its appearance was virtually the same as the previous models.

In the early 1950s a boy and a girl golliwog (*pages 118-19*) were produced in the *Evripoze* range. Both were made of quality felt; the girl wore a fixed yellow blouse, red jacket and short blue skirt with red and white socks, red shoes and she stood about 18 inches high. The boy wore a fixed yellow waistcoat with a green jacket and red trousers. There were two main types of these *Evripoze* dolls. The *Evripoze* golliwog (number A405) had either four open or closed fingers. Some had ten buttons, others only seven. The open-fingered version had ten buttons, a blue jacket, a yellow waistcoat, red trousers, rolling-disc eyes and a white felt bow tie. It was advertised at 24 inches but they are closer to 20 inches. The red felt mouth has white thread sewn across the centre.

During the 1950s Dean's produced the *Turipoze* types of dolls as well as the traditional variety. Seven buttons were used on this model, number A405.

Some dolls had plastic 'lock-in' eyes, while others had the rolling-disc type. Different colours also helped to create a variety of different personalities. There were size, colour and accessory variations in both types of golliwog. The stock numbers were also different. Here are a few variations of colours and buttons.

It is important to note that just as other manufacturers such as Merrythought and Wendy Boston, would alter the appearance of a golliwog by using different colours, fabrics and accessories, Dean's did too, often due to stock availability.

The closed finger type has seven buttons, still plastic lock-in eyes, green jacket, yellow waistcoat, red trousers, white silk bow tie and is about 20 inches high.

In the 'traditional' variety (numbers 402, 401 and 407), the sizes varied as well as the number of buttons. Late 1950s golliwogs, had different numbers: 5059, 12 inches; 5060, 15 inches and 5061, 19 inches. The *Evripoze* model retained the same number 405.

An important change occurred with Dean's traditional golliwogs in 1961. The company began to use a sailcloth fabric instead of the more expensive felt. Dean's maintained that felt was less durable and the new material could be washed. It was also hard wearing and less susceptible to moths. This 'new' golliwog was stuffed with terylene and the eyes were of the plastic lock-in types. It retained the felt jacket which was removable for washing, while the waistcoat and trousers were printed on to the fabric. Some of the trousers were red and white striped, others were solid red. The red and white trousers were used on the *Chime* golliwog dolls *(right)*. The new stock numbers were 801 (12 inches), 802 (15 inches) and 803 (19 inches). The wig was now a deep pile plush and the doll had seven buttons. The colours were traditional: blue jackets, yellow waistcoat, red trousers, and white bow tie. Although these golliwogs look cheaply made, as compared with the earlier Dean's felt dolls, they are not. The sailcloth used to makes these dolls is very durable and if cared for, they will last a lifetime.

1962 saw the same dolls and stock numbers. The only difference was that the wig was long pile plush instead of the shorter type.

This doll *(opposite)* was also made with the durable sailcloth and used the same traditional colours of blue, red, yellow and white. In 1963 the company continued the same stock except 803 was now the only doll with long pile plush wigs and 19 inches. 801 and 802 reverted to a shorter deep pile plush.

In 1965 new changes were introduced. Dolls 801 (13 inches) and 802 (16 inches) sported three buttons, two on the jacket and one on the yellow printed waistcoat. 803 at 20 inches still had seven buttons. Two new gollys were introduced: No 829 at 19 inches was *Molligog*, the golliwog's girlfriend: 830, 20 inches, the *Chime* golliwogs. Basically it was a traditional golliwog with a musical chime implant. The trousers were red and white striped.

A most unusual golliwog was made by Dean's in 1966. The first ever, white-faced

(*Left*) Chime golliwogs

801, 12 inches

802, 15 inches

803, 19 inches

1961

(*Below left*) As above but with long pile plush wig, 1962

(*Below*) Photograph from 1963 catalogue. The largest is 19 inches high with long pile plush wig. The other two have short pile wigs

(*Bottom*) Photograph from 1965 catalogue showing golliwogs ref: 801, 802, 803, 829, 830

Synthetic pile wig

Joggle eyes

Felt face, mouth and body

Ribbon bow tie (missing)

5 button type

Mr Smith Snr & Mr Smith Jnr
First ever white-faced golliwog, 2 sizes, 1966

Synthetic pile wig
Plastic lock-in eyes
Sailcloth face and body
Ribbon tie (missing)
Jacket (missing)

golliwog to be produced by a toy manufacturer. Presented in two sizes, it was called *Mr. Smith Senior* and *Mr. Smith Junior*, at 16 inches and 13 inches respectively. They were virtually the same as the traditional black versions, with the same fabric and colour scheme, except the face was white with white cloth buttons for the eyes and nose.

The London buying office had faced problems selling the traditional golliwog in the USA at a time when black people were fighting for civil rights and against racist beliefs, practices and imagery. So, the manager suggested that the firm should make a golliwog with a white face. Dean's went ahead with the idea and made a sample which was approved by everyone and soon the doll went into production.

In an effort to name the golliwog, Dean's proposed to call it *Mr. Smith* after David Smith the manager who suggested the idea initially. Unfortunately this coincided with the time when Mr. Ian Smith, the prime minister of Rhodesia (now Zimbabwe), had declared UDI (Unilateral Declaration of Independence) from Great Britain and the Commonwealth.

Although there was no intention of associating Dean's golliwog with this event, press reports from across the world highlighted the white-faced doll and caused a stir. Those who own one have a valuable product as only some 100 of the *Mr. Smith* gollys were made and most went to America.

Dean's traditional golliwogs changed very little in 1969. 800, 802 and 803 were identical to the previous 1965 issues with 800 being the smallest size. The *Chime Golly* now had red trousers with a polka dotted bow tie and stood at 20 inches. The main difference was the eyes, which were of the metal or plastic lock-in type with painted pupils. Around the same time the firm re-introduced a printed rag golliwog based on the 1920s style. Given stock number 160, it had a plush wig, printed clothing and features. In the late 1980s Dean's introduced a felt golly based on their dolls of the 1930s and 1940s. This doll has rolling disc eyes, traditional colours (blue, red, yellow) with a white bow tie and a black short pile synthetic wig.

The latest 'traditional golly' made in 1993 is based on patterns from the 1960s versions. They are made in brightly-coloured felt and sail cloth. One feature which differs from the 1960s version is a bulbous nose. They also have woollen yarn wigs, disc eyes, red and white trousers with a bow tie. These are amongst the best gollies Dean's produced.

Synthetic wig
Plastic lock-in eyes
Printed features
Ribbon tie
Sailcloth body
Felt jacket
Single button

Left: Mr Golly, a 1980s version of the early Dean's golliwog of printed rag

Below: Another 1980s reproduction of Dean's early rag golliwogg, with synthetic wig and printed features and clothing

Synthetic pile wig

Felt face

Ribbon bow-tie

Felt clothing & body

Synthetic wig

Felt face

Ribbon bow-tie

Felt clothing & body

Traditional golly, 1993
stock numbers 042245-18"
042246-14"

Merrythought Toy Co.

The Merrythought Toy Company was founded
in 1919 when WG Homes and GH Laton
formed an alliance with the launch of their
humble spinning mill in Yorkshire. They made
yarn from crude mohair imported from South
Africa, Turkey and elsewhere. However, the
popularity of mohair waned during the early
1920s, due to the development of cheap
synthetic fibres which were more in demand.
Around this time Dyson Hall & Co, operating in
Huddersfield, also found its business crippled
by synthetic fibres. Its factory was bought by
the Laton Holmes partnership.

The illustration below depicts a golliwog
made in 1932 by Merrythought. It is almost
identical to the Chad Valley dolls (of the same
period), except this doll wears a more tailored
outfit. The jacket is longer in the sleeve and
white gloves are worn as well as trousers.

Lambskin wig

Painted linen button eyes

Painted nose & mouth

Buckram face

Felt collar

Ribbon tie

Brass buttons

Silk plush body

Felt hands

Plastic-coated heavy canvas feet

*This is the first silk plush
golliwog from Merrythought
Cotton filled. 16 inches high
No. 51147, 1932*

*Far left: Clinton Derricks'
drawing of a Merrythought doll
of 1932*

The clothing is made of velvet (jacket and trousers) and felt (waistcoat, gloves and collar). It has a mohair wig, painted linen button eyes, felt mouth, painted nose and heavy cotton body.

Sheepskin was also used for wigs on these early Merrythought golliwogs.

I believe this doll, like the silk plush model only dressed, was definitely made in 1932, but there seems to be no stock number assigned to golliwogs produced in that year. It was a special model made for various stores and shops as a display for promotions and is even rarer than the S1147 model.

In pursuit of a market for their mohair yarns and fabrics, Laxton-Holmes hired two men – AC Janisc, then head of sales at the toy company JK Farnell and CJ Rendel, then head of production at Chad Valley. They became directors of the company. Holmes-Laxton leased a building from the Coalbrookdale Company at Ironbridge, Shropshire in 1930, to produce toys made of mohair and other fabrics. The toy company began to trade as 'Merrythought', a name which derived from 'wishbone', the breastbone of a fowl, which when pulled apart, awards the one holding the bigger half his or her wish – or 'Merrythought'.

As a result of Mr Rendle's departure, other employees left Chad Valley for Merrythought, one of whom was Florence Atwood, a deaf mute designer who studied design at the Deaf and Dumb School of Manchester. Florence honed her skills under the designer, Norah Wellings, who herself was also at Chad Valley before leaving to form her own company.

In 1931 Florence Atwood created the complete selection of soft toys for the first Merrythought line. Among her creations as well as those of other artists were Lawson Wood's 'monkeys' and MGM's 'Jerry Mouse'. But the very first doll made by Florence was the golliwog in 1932. It was available in three sizes, the smallest was 16 inches and the largest was 22 inches. With a stock number of S1147 and made of art silk plush, these dolls are very rare indeed. The design was derived from the Chad Valley golliwog – 'Wally Wag' of the late 1920s.

Mohair wig

Velveteen face

Plastic eyes

Painted mouth

Ribbon tie

Silk plush body

Felt pads (worn)

Slumber golliwog

1936

Another version of the silk plush golliwog is the, 'slumber' doll made in 1934. The doll shown on page 131 was made around 1936 and with its plastic inserted eyes is slightly different to the 1934 model which had painted linen eyes. Merrythought dolls have variants, as do Chad Valley and Dean's.

Although the Chad Valley doll is rare, the chances of finding one are greater because they were already in production by 1932. In 1934 Merrythought introduced the 'slumber' range of soft toys, one of which was the golliwog. This doll was also a carryover from Chad Valley with very minor differences. Also made of art silk plush, the slumber golliwog came in various sizes from 36 to 13 inches. With the stock number 1276, its colours were a pastel arrangement – light blue for the jacket, yellow for the waistcoat and rose pink for the trousers. It also has a voice-box in the middle of its chest.

In 1936 and 1937, Merrythought produced a golliwog for two consecutive years. Number 1345 came in five sizes ranging from 25 inches to 14 inches. Because the stock number is different from the golliwog in 1932 and 1933, this doll was somewhat different from earlier versions. It had glass eyes set in and two dots on the ankles.

The next golliwog made by the company came in 1949 (CN1345), with eyes similar to number 1345, but with a 'fitted voice' which was actually a chime. It had different eyes and spats and was an export model. This same year was also the debut of Merrythoughts' *Jollywogs* (4807) in sizes ranging from 16 to 12 inches.

Jollywog dolls are one of the most vividly striking golliwogs ever made by Merrythought. You will not find them in great numbers, but one might turn up if you persevere.

Their production continued through to 1955. These *Jollywogs* were made of a strong black Italian fabric with removable clothes: satin printed trousers and a colourful felt jacket and waistcoat. The face was moulded buckram with applied or painted features; the clothing was also removable. With black or gray wigs, these dolls made quite stunning golliwogs. The *Jollywogs* were designed by Florence

Mohair wig

Linen button eyes

Painted nose & mouth

Collar, tie & pom poms

Felt pads

Slumber *golliwog*

Kapok filled

13 inches high

1934

Jollywogs
Designed by Florence Attwood
12 to 16 inches high
1949

Synthetic wig
Painted features
Buckram face
Cotton collar
Felt tie
Felt jacket & waistcoat
Italian cotton body
Sateen trousers

Jolliwogs are one of the
most vividly striking
golliwogs ever made
by Merrythought

This Jolliwog is also rare, even
more so because it has a grey
wig

Atwood and were her last golliwog designs for Merrythought.

The *Lucky Sam* doll is one of the *Famous Artist Design* line, created by artist, GE Studdy, for Merrythought in 1938. A most unusual golliwog-type character, with its orange-red hair, chubby stature, and trousers sporting horseshoes on each leg. It is made mostly of felt, except for the face which looks formed. *Lucky Sam* came only in one size of 9 inches and was possibly kapok filled.

Unfortunately, many of the records of these earlier types of dolls are lost or were destroyed in the flooding of the factory by the Severn River in 1946.

In 1953 the company produced golliwog 5219, which was the forerunner to the later felt golliwog. It was designed by Jean Barber, the new head designer for the company after Florence's death. The sizes were 24, 19 and 15 inches. It came with a blue jacket, red trousers, rolling disc eyes and a yellow waist-coat. The clothing was not removable and the doll had wired limbs which enabled it to pose.

This poseable golliwog is rare. Almost identical to the Dean's *Evripoze* line of the 1950s, it has a plush wig, joggle eyes, with a felt mouth, jacket, shirt, waistcoat, legs and feet. The buttons on the jacket are brass while those on the waistcoat are plastic. The tie could also be made of felt.

Around the same time the firm introduced 'Mollywog' a girlfriend for the boy doll. It is important to note that many of the Dean's and Merrythought golliwogs were very similar during the 1930s through to the 1950s. So, it is no surprise that the Merrythought *Mollywog* looks virtually like the Dean's *Wolligog*. *Mollywog* stood at about 22 inches, was made entirely of felt with a wool wig, painted metal disc eyes, yellow blouse, red jacket, blue skirt, red shoes and blue and white polka dot socks.

The two golliwogs *(opposite)* are late 1950s all-felt dolls. Buttons and ties are often missing. Some have felt eyes or painted metal eyes, painted mouths or felt mouths, rayon ties or felt ties, long pile wigs or short pile; the combinations vary.

Lucky Sam *No. 1686*

Designer: GE Studdy

1938

Mohair wig

Formed face

Painted features

Felt shirt, waistcoat, trousers

& feet

Golliwog no. 5219

Designer: Jean Barber

15, 19, 24 inches high

1953

Between 1954 and 1959, Merrythought created a golliwog (number 1932) in four sizes – 36, 19, 15 and 12 inches. Also in 1955, a golliwog pajama case was introduced.

Another, larger all-felt golliwog *(above)* has a rather whimsical face. Every golliwog doll has its own character, some more pronounced than others. Again, the tie and buttons are missing yet it still is a vivid, exciting and striking doll. It has a plush wig, painted metal eyes, felt mouth, and the entire body is felt.

The doll *(left)* is a *Chime* golliwog from around 1967. It is 20 inches high and kapok stuffed. With a plush wig, the doll is made

Mollywog
All felt
1950s

Plush wig
Felt eyes
Painted mouth
Felt body

Golliwog
Late 1950s

Plush wig
Painted metal eyes
Felt mouth
Felt body

Plush wig
Painted metal eyes
Felt mouth & body

Plush wig
Felt eyes & body
Painted mouth

Golliwog
All felt, c.1960s
(Sally Letham collection)

Chime golliwog
Kapok stuffed
20 inches high
c.1967

completely of velveteen, with clear plastic eyes, felt mouth (not original), rayon tie and plastic buttons. There was no jacket on this particular model, but other models of the same period are found have jackets.

An example of the 'jointed' golliwog is *(right)* 19 inches high, cotton-stuffed, with a blue jacket (they also come with red jackets). Many of the golliwogs made in the early 1930s were lost or destroyed during World War II. Also quite a few of the late 1950s to 1960s golliwogs were discarded because of the controversy over the political correctness of the golliwog taking place at that time. So, although they are not extremely rare, you still will not find the fairs or shops full of them.

Jointed golliwog
Cotton stuffed
19 inches high

Plush wig
Painted metal eyes
Felt mouth
Cotton jacket, waistcoat &
trousers
Plastic buttons
Flannel feet

Plush wig

Felt eyes & mouth

Cotton face

Cotton jacket & trousers

Plastic buttons

Flannel feet

Jointed golliwog

12 inches high

1960s

In 1960 the first golliwog doll made was number 143 in sizes 36, 19, 15 and 12 inches. One year later a cotton golliwog (192) without the jacket was produced. It had only one year of production. A nylon golliwog at 6 inches was part of the line in 1962. In 1964 the company made a 'jointed' golliwog, (344). Only the head was jointed, which could turn 360 degrees. Its sizes ranged from 19 to 12 inches, and it had a red or blue jacket, with painted metal fixed eyes, cotton-stuffed and a yellow waistcoat.

Here is 12-inch example of the 'jointed' golliwog, cotton-stuffed, and just as difficult to find as other dolls of this period. Possibly because of the smaller size, or lack of materials, some of these dolls have felt instead of metal eyes. That same year the company introduced the new 'minstrel' doll, which was basically their golliwog with a top hat. The popularity of the TV series, *The Black and White Minstrel Show*, probably encouraged the company to make these dolls.

Minstrel golliwogs
Variations in material used
for different sizes.
Cotton & kapok stuffed.
1960s

Plush wig
Felt or metal eyes
Felt mouth
Cotton body &
clothing

Cotton sailcloth tie & legs

Plastic buttons

Felt jacket & feet

Lanky Joe, a tall minstrel doll with long legs was offered at 35 and 21 inches in height. The minstrel doll (346) did not look at all like the minstrel doll of 1939 called *Kentucky Minstrel,* which looked more like Norah Wellings' *Island Dolls* of the same period. *Lanky Joe* was added to the range in 1965 and 1966.

Two *Lanky Joe* golliwogs, *(left)* in the only colours available, blue and red. The blue model is 21 inches and the red model is 35 inches. The jacket on the taller doll was repaired and the buttons placed incorrectly on the doll. They should appear as on the smaller doll. The taller doll was rescued from a dump. They are not easy to find.

Lanky Joe *golliwogs*

Colours: blue & red

21 & 35 inches high

1960s

Felt hat & mouth

Plush wig

Painted metal eyes

Velveteen face, hands & torso

Cotton sailcloth legs

Glove Golly

1967

Chime golliwog

1967

The second *Chime* golliwog, ranging from 38 to 12 inches was created in 1967 and was in production until 1985. With a stock number 484, this golliwog resembled the other popular golliwogs produced by the company during that period. Red or blue jacket, painted metal eyes, felt and cotton fabric with black and white striped trousers. Also in 1967 the *Glove Golly* made its debut (527) with stuffed head and hands. The colours and fabrics were the same as the dolls.

Social unrest in America in the late 1960s and early 1970s, aided the production demise of golliwogs by all major companies. Demand dwindled as they became less popular.

Plush wig

Painted metal eyes

Velveteen face & hands

Felt mouth

Sailcloth tie & trousers

Plastic buttons

Cotton waistcoat

Modern mohair golliwog
14 inches high
Limited edition of 500

Plush wig
Velvet face, hands & feet
Clear plastic eyes
Formed nose
Synthetic foam mouth
Cotton-laced shirt
Velvet jacket & trousers
Brass buttons
Braided silk cord seam

Velvet golliwog
18 inches high
1986

However, in the late 1970s and early 1980s, the golliwog made a comeback due to development of a collector's market. The golliwog became so popular, especially among Americans, that many have left Britain for the United States.

Golliwogs are still made by Merrythought today. There is the *Velvet Golly* (D89A1), 18 inches high, with or without a chime, *Golly in Mohair* (300A0), 14 inches high (limited edition of 500) and the 15-inch golliwog (135A1). Just recently another limited edition was produced – *Jolly Golly*. Merrythought golliwogs are still made with attention to old fashioned quality which is often lacking in other golliwogs today.

Two versions of 135Al date from 1989, one with a jacket and one without. Both are 15 inches high. Merrythought dolls are foam filled, made of velveteen and doubleknit fabric, have plush wigs of rayon and artificial suede mouths. The eyes are clear plastic, the buttons of plastic and they have formed noses.

Black dolls by Merrythought include:

Dixie Bebe
(*Jolly Piccaninny*, 12 61) circa 1930s

Topsy
No. 1566 made in 1937-38

Chef Yah Sah
No. 1567 made in 1937-38

Jose
No. 1809 made in 1939

Kentucky Minstrel
No. 1810 made in 1939

Sambo
No. 1811 made in 1938, 1945, 1950-55

Dixie (Picaninny)
No. CE1261 made in 1947

Black Mammy
No. 4623 made in 1950- 54

Lucky Sam
No. 1686

Versions of 1351A
15 inches high
1989

Pedigree Soft Toys

Pedigree was initially established during the middle of the 19th century as G & J Lines Ltd in London by the founders, George and Joseph Lines. The brothers produced baby carriages and wooden toys and when Joseph's sons, William, Walter and Arthur, returned from World War I, they resolved not to return to the family business. Instead, they decided to make pedal cars, dolls, scooters, dolls houses and prams in their own modern factory. The premises was located in Ormside Street, Old Kent Road, London. Soon they were inundated with orders from many outlets keen to purchase such quality items. By 1924 production was so good that the firm was a to expand to Merton near Wimbledon. Boasting the largest factory in Great Britain, the familiar triangular trademark of Lines Bros. Limited was adopted in 1927. Other factories were acquired so that clockwork toys and model aircraft could be produced. Around this time and into the early 1930's Lines Bros. was doing so well that purchasing most of the Hamleys Toy Store shares kept the store from closing down. Hamleys had never fully recovered from rebuilding their premises at Regent Street in 1900. Also in the early 30's, the trademark *Pedigree* was registered for prams. In 1933 the company became a public company and soon brought in chemists and scientific researchers to develop and test ideas for toys, paints and materials. The first dolls, were made in the 1930's of celluloid and cellulose acetate and in 1937 Pedigree Soft Toys published its first catalogue.

During World War II the company made guns, land mine cases, shell cases, pack saddles, rocket propelled aircraft and other items of war. In 1940 during a raid on London, the factory at Merton was bombed and extensively damaged, yet none of the 7,000 workers was injured throughout the war.

Pedigree golly
Sailcloth fabric
Plastic eyes & mouth
c.1960s
(Sally Letham collection)

Pedigree golly
Sailcloth fabric
Plastic eyes & mouth
23 inches high
c.1960s
(Sally Letham collection)

Solly Golly
Cotton filled
c.1950s and 1960s

Medium pile wig
Plastc lock-in eyes
Velveteen face
Plastc lock-in mouth
Lace collar
Corduroy jacket
Sateen waistcoat
Brass buttons
Cotton tartan trousers
Velveteen feet

Pile wig
Cotton face & hands
Felt eyes & mouth
Tie (not original)
Buttons (not original)
Felt jacket
Corduroy trousers
Cotton feet

After the war years and the purchase of Joy Toys in Australia, Lines Bros. built a factory in Northern Ireland and merged International Model Aircraft with Pedigree Soft Toys. By 1955 the firm had moved all soft toy production to Belfast. Around 1966 the Belfast factory closed and soft toy manufacture moved to Canterbury, England. But it was around the mid to late 1950s when most of the Pedigree golliwogs which can be found today were produced, ranging from the 23-inch talking *Jolly Golly* to the 12-inch soft doll. The talking golliwog wears a blue corduroy jacket with a yellow felt flower sewn onto the lapel. This golliwog was the most elegant of the Pedigree range. Pedigree golly sizes varied and all looked similar, but none looked as elaborate as this talking model. Many of the golliwog range had plastic eyes and mouths, while cheaper models used felt and cheaper fabric for clothing. Sizes range enormously, from around 32 inches to 12 inches.

These golliwogs *(below)* from the late 1950s and early 1960s are the only Pedigree models seen at fairs and in retail outlets in recent years. If there were any produced earlier or later, they have not been recorded. In the 1970s the company and its subsidiaries faltered and were taken over by the Dunbee-Combex-Marx conglomeration, but by 1988 the Canterbury factory had closed down.

Solly Golly

Cotton filled,

16 inches high,

c.1950s

Solly Golly

Cotton filled,

Made in art silk plush

16 inches high

c.1950s

Pile wig

Plastic lock-in eyes

Plastic lock-in mouth

Cotton face & body

Felt jacket

Pile wig

Plastic lock-in eyes

Cotton velveteen face

Plastic lock-in mouth

Cotton waistcoat

Brass buttons

Solly Golly

Cotton filled

Felt flowers on lapel

c.1950s

Solly Golly

Probably the largest

Pedigree golliwog made

Cotton filled

32 inches high

c.1950s

Synthetic wig

Velveteen face,

hands & feet

Felt eyes & mouth

Metal buttons

Felt jacket

Cotton trousers

Pelham Puppets

In 1947 Bob Pelham started creating puppets suitable for children. After demonstrating his puppets at Hamleys, the largest toy store in London, he distributed them to toy shops that had never sold these types of puppets before. The toys were so well received that Bob had one of the girls on his staff permanently demonstrating the puppets at the store. She worked there for seven years. Meanwhile, the range was growing, starting with the 'standard puppets' which had round wooden heads, painted features, and the strings to control the head, hands, knees and back. They included the *Dutch Boy and Girl, Clown, Rupert the Bear* and the *Golliwog*.

Standard golliwogs

SL type

13 inches high

1950s

Fur wig

Wooden head & body

Painted features

Painted metal pin nose

Ribbon bow tie

Cotton clothing

Metal mitten hands

Fur wig

Wooden head

Painted metal pin nose

Wooden eyes & mouth

Felt bow tie

Clay hands

Wooden body

Cotton clothing

Later the company introduced the SL range which was controlled in the same manner, but had moulded composition heads with realistic features. They included *Pinocchio*, *Prince Charming*, *Cinderella* and others.

Soon came the SM models which had moving mouths, one of which was the *Witch*, but less known is the large golliwog in top hat and tails with moving mouth. This is one of the rarer golliwog toys because it is more difficult to operate for little children. It is a stunning toy, brightly coloured with real fur hair. When found, it may have the top hat missing, but is still desirable.

Golliwog, SM type
(Top hat missing)

Fur wig
Painted eyes
Wooden nose, face & body
Movable mouth
Fixed cotton bow tie
Sateen waist coat
Rayon jacket & trousers
Metal hands

Pelham Puppets
Woodenhead *puppet*
One wooden bar for very
young children

Painted features
Metal pin nose
Wooden face & body
Clay hands
Cotton clothing

Synthetic wig
Wooden face, hands & body
Felt eyes & mouth
Cotton clothing

'Junior puppets' had short strings and were less difficult to operate. Made for children from to five to six years, it also included the golliwog. For those children too young to operate string puppets there was the wooden head line, a simple wooden puppet with one bar which made the puppet jump up and down.

Through the 1960s and 1970s the company thrived and added new characters such as *Ermintrude*, *Florence* and *Dougal* from the *Magic Roundabout*, along with all the Walt Disney Favorites. In 1975 the *Vent Puppet* was created for youngsters who wanted to try ventriloquist techniques. One hand would hold the control for the mouth and head, while the other would become the doll's own hand.

In the 1980s more characters were created including the *Peanuts* characters and many of the *Muppets*. Always recognizing a winning TV character as selling potential, the company has continued to reign supreme. Today Pelham Puppets are still sold all over the world.

Standard golliwog
SL type,
13 inches high
c.1970s

Fur wig
Wooden head & body
Painted features & metal nose
Felt bow tie
Cotton clothing
Metal hands

Standard golliwog
13 inches
1940s to 1950s

Straw hat
Painted features
Felt bow tie
Rayon suit
Metal mitten hands

Allwin (Richards Son Allwin)

Allwin was established in 1924 at Sidway Works, Granville Street, Birmingham, moving to Great Bridge, Tipton, Staffs in 1936. Makers of dolls, their line contained over 100 types of doll including mascots, character and cuddly dolls. One of the range was *Rigmel Green Golliwog* a character from the children's book *The Fairy's Password*. The name *Allwin* was the company's trademark. The *Rigmel* golliwog, made in 1936, was entirely of felt. Its facial features were painted on, except the nose, which was a painted wooden ball, locked into the face. Mohair sewn onto the head, gave it a long curly mane. The body was of green felt, with white stripes sewn onto the legs. Four shell buttons were attached to the jacket which had two orange patches on either sleeve. The bow tie and shoes were orange felt. The clothing was one unit with tails attached at the lower back which were unremovable. The 18 inch doll was jointed at the waist.

Allwin

Ringmel green golliwog

18 inches high, 1936

Mohair wig

Painted eyes, mouth

wooden nose

Velvet face, suit & hands

Shell buttons

Felt bow-tie, strips & feet

Atlas Manufacturing Co.

Located at Stanley Row, Woodford, London, this company produced golliwogs, teddy-bears and other soft toys from around 1914. The dolls were made simply and the animals were dressed in various outfits. The golliwogs were stuffed with wood-wool, wore rabbit fur wigs, had shoe button eyes, ribbon tie bound by a metal clip with black white check trousers attached to red jacket without tails. Produced in two sizes; price 1/6d. The example below has a fur wig, shoe-button eyes, formed nose of treated linen, a cotton threaded mouth, ribbon tie with metal clip, a paper collar, white jointed arms, flannel jacket, linen trousers and treated linen feet.

This is another rare doll and highly sought after. Because the materials used are not as durable as some of the other early examples, many perished.

Bendy Toys

In 1953, the Newfeld Ltd Co. in Ashford, Middlesex, introduced the *Bendy* dolls and toys made of foam rubber with a tough wire skeleton concealed in the body. The same principal applied to Dean's early *Evripoze* dolls. The founder Charles Neufeld was an avid chemistry expert and worked at the Dunlop laboratory experimenting with latex rubber. In 1948, Charles and his brother Helmuth started the firm in Chelsea, then Hayes and Hackney. In 1953 the firm moved to Ashford. After their success with foam rubber, a designer friend, Ray Mitchell, created the *Bendy Bunny* and due to its success, the firm launched their first toys. Many other characters were made including many of Walt Disney fame, along with many advertising characters from Britain and America. Woolworths was instrumental in the success of these toys, especially in Britain.

In 1963 a fire destroyed part of the Bendy factory, but with worldwide sales at an all-time high, the firm still prospered, mainly because of extensive publicity at trade shows, fairs and large stores.

The firm's ability to be innovative kept it in the public eye. Millions of toys were sold over the years and by 1973 the company celebrated its silver jubilee. During the late 1970s and early 1980s every character imaginable was made by Bendy Toys. There were *Mickey, Donald* and *Pluto* and the *Pink Panther* from Disney. The line also included *Bugs Bunny, Matilda, Popeye, Rupert, Bendy Bunny, Tom & Jerry, Peanuts, the Muppets* and many more. They ranged in size from 7 to 23 inches and the display sizes could be as high as 9 feet.

Mabel Bland-Hawkes

In business around 1918 in Lavender Hill, London SW11, the firm designed and made soft dolls and mascots. Mabel received a patent on 15 May 1918 for her articulated limbs on soft bodied dolls. In 1921, the firm produced the lightweight *Fairies and Father Christmas* dolls, with others in their range. By 1923 the firm had added *Baby Royal*, a life sized baby doll, *Little Lady Anne* and *Tutenkamen*, an Egyptian golliwog mascot doll. There are no pictures available of the *Tutenkamen* doll, which probably looked quite human but was called a golliwog because Egyptians were considered black by the British. At the same time, Mabel acquired a patent for her floating, washable, jointed cuddly toy. The firm went on to produce other dolls and toys through the early 1930s.

Bendy Golly
11-13 inches high,
1956

Britannia Toy Co.

Originally called Mark Robin & Co. after the name of its founder, the business began as Britannia Toy Works in 1914/1915. Based at 9/11 Worship Street, London EC2, and later at 87 Great Eastern Street, London EC2, they were in the business of wholesale and export, and in 1943 moved into the Alliance Works, Windus Road, London, producing dolls and toys. Over the years the firm was a success until the end of World War II when they ceased to trade.

The *Britannia Golliwog (below)* came with a long pile wig, plastic face, joggle eyes, painted mouth and a rayon plush suit.

The Britannia Golliwog
with voicebox
Woodwool stuffed, 14 inches high, c.1940s

British United Toy Manufacturing Co.

This firm began operations in 1912 with their factory at Union Works, Southey Road, South Tottenham, Middlesex and had their showroom

British United Toy Manufacturing
Omega trademark

at 118 Fore Street, Cripplegate, London EC2. It was a maker of a animals such as *Spit Fire*, the lucky variety of dolls and toys including cat, musical bunny, barking beggar and other plush toys. By 1927 the firm, using the trademark *Omega*, had both factory and showrooms at Union Works, Carysfort Road, Stoke Newington N16. They made gollys in striped jacket and trousers, fur wigs, shoe button eyes, stitched mouth and ribbon bow tie. They had the soft toy structure and are very rare. This doll was available in 1927 along with animals on wheels, coaster toys, teddy bears and other items produced by the company.

British United Toy
Manufacturing golliwog 1927

Burbank Toys

From the Dundee/Combex/Marx group, this firm produced dolls for only a few years and made many fairy tale and nursery rhyme characters as well as talking stuffed dolls and puppets, one of which was a talking golliwog made in 1976. It was 26 inches high and stuffed with foam and cotton. The eyes were wooden balls locked in on top of white felt. The face was felt and the body was made of a stretch knit. The red torso was covered by a blue waistcoat, while the legs were yellow striped with flared bottoms. It is not known if there were any other models of golliwogs from Burbank, but because the company was so short-lived, it is doubtful. Although the firm stopped production in 1977, their remainder stock was still being sold three years later.

JA Burman (Fondle Toys)

From 1919, the firm was producing dolls and toys at 32 Whitecross Street, London EC1. Its line, *Zoo Toy Co*, included jointed dolls, dressed and undressed mascots and plush toys. In the late 1930s the firm's brand name became Fondle Toys at their new address of 911 London Lane, London E8. One of the toys made in the 1930s was a soft golliwog doll with polka dot trousers, a bright jacket with a large white collar and bow tie. It is difficult to find much information on these golliwogs by Fondle Toys because very little reference material exists. The company changed its name to Fondle Toys Ltd in the mid-1950s and moved to 440 Kingshand Road, Hackney, London.

Burbank Toys talking golliwog, 1976

Fondle Toys golliwog

Chiltern golliwog
Cotton filled with felt and
sailcloth clothes
12 inches high
Plastic nose & eyes, c.1960s
(Sally Letham collection)

Chiltern Toys (HG Stone & Co.)

Chiltern Toy Works was founded as early as 1908. That year the firm produced the *Evening News Doll* for a newspaper business which wanted to show that dolls could be made successfully in Britain. The factory was in Chesham, Buckinghamshire, near the Chiltern Hills. Focusing on the construction of plush toys, the *Evening News Dolls*, which were about 10 inches high, had a pink cambric body, china head and a mohair wig. Many were sold but cheaper dolls from Germany flooded the market and the doll was dropped.

In 1912 to 1914, Mr Leon Rees, patented his dolls' eyes which were attached loosely on vertical points in a doll's head. He patented his turning head by fitting the head and neck into a hemispherical cup in the body. In 1920 he founded the firm L Rees & Co. and was later joined by Mr HG Stone the owner of Chiltern Toy Works. With the new factory in Tottenham, London, they traded under the name HG Stone & Co.

In 1923 Mr. Rees registered the trademark *Heather-Belle* for toys and dolls. Over the years a broad range of soft toys was created from infants' cuddly toys to great plush animals on wheels, but no rag dolls.

By 1946 the firm moved to Pontypool in Wales and produced the plastic dolls made by Nene Plastics of Raunds Northants. HG Stone had the sole selling rights of Nenes' registered *Rosebud* line.

The remaining years were spent making plastic or vinyl dolls of excellent quality; fewer soft toys where produced. In 1967 the firm was acquired by Chad Valley, becoming Chiltern-Chad Valley lines.

JK Farnell & Co.

In 1840, John K Farnell began his family business in Notting Hill, London making pin-cushions, pen wipers and tea cosies. After his death in 1897 the family moved the company to Acton, to a house called The Elms where they made soft toys from rabbit skins and later from other less expensive materials. By the early 1920s the firm was registered as a private limited business, building a factory next to The Elms and taking on more employees. In 1925 the name Alpha which had been used for a number of years, officially became the trademark. Then the company expanded its market throughout the US, Canada and Europe. In the early 1930s the company was thriving until 1934 when a fire destroyed the factory and stock. In 1935, a new factory was built and three new lines were introduced including *Che-Kee* (lambswool); *Alpac* (Alpaca) and *Joy Day* dolls. Along with the earlier lines, *Alpha* and *Teddy*, the business was back on its feet, opening showrooms at 1 New Union Street, London EC2. In 1940 the factory was bombed again in the Blitz and later rebuilt. Many of the dolls made during the 1930s were of excellent quality and artistry. Little is known about the rare Farnell golliwogs due mainly to lost records. If any were made by the firm during the 1950s and 1960s they must have been produced in small numbers compared to other well known companies during the same period. In 1968 Farnell was bought by a finance company and ceased to trade in the mid 1970s.

J & G Franklin & Sons

Located at 11-17 Godstone Crescent, Dalston, London E8, this maker produced rubber dolls in 1920. Using the trademark *Rubbadubdub*, it offered items such as *Charlie Chaplin*, *Funny Finny* (fish), *Dinkie Dutchie* (Dutch girl), *Humpty Dumpty*, *Jack Drake* (duck), *King Swan*, *Cock-a-doodle doo*, *Sunny Jim* and *Uncle Tom* (golliwog); all were floating toys.

Franklin & Sons Uncle Tom

AJ Halliday Co.

As early as 1916, this company was producing dolls, toys, games and fancy wares at 32/33 Aldermanbury, London EC2. Under the *Givejoy* trademark their dolls came fully jointed with glass eyes, fixed or sleeping. Golliwogs were of the early type with large noses and are very rare indeed.

Hammond Manufacturing Co.

Established around 1915 with the office and factory at Mosely Street, Burton-on-Trent, this company made games, dolls, bears and toys. All the dolls were made on the premises except for the heads. Dolls were stuffed with materials from the company's own mill. In 1916 the dolls had fixed and moving eyes as well as still and jointed bodies. Golliwogs were produced in 1917 and the firm continued to make porcelain, rag and composition dolls.

Hermann-Spielwaren GmbH

Johann Hermann, the founder and grandfather of the present director was residing in Neufang before World War I, a small village near Sonneberg. Like most people in the area, Johann produced toys in a small workshop, helped by his six children. During this time in the US, plush bears were all the rage, causing even greater demand. So, around 1913, Arthur, Adelheid and Max, three of Johann's children, started making the first Hermann teddy bears in Sonneberg, the toy capital of the world. When Johann died in 1919, the youngest son Max founded his own company for teddy bear manufacture. By 1923 he had moved the firm to Sonneberg and with new orders from America the business expanded. Max's teddies were exported in their thousands to all parts of the world. In 1945, after the division of Germany, Thuringia, with Sonneberg its capital fell under Soviet rule. In 1947, Max's son Rolf-

Gerhard joined the firm and by 1949 they had founded Hermann & Co. KG, in Coburg, in the American occupied zone, twenty minutes away from Sonneberg. By 1953 the entire firm had moved to Coburg with all tangible assets left in Sonneberg. Max Hermann died in 1955 and since then, after nearly forty years of political stability, the company has thrived. Today the line of plush toys comprises more than five hundred different models, with large numbers sold each year.

Henry J Hughes & Sons

Located at 98-100 Tottenham Road, Kingsland, London N1, this firm was making dolls, rattles and soft toys from 1887. In 1909 they made rag dolls and wooden toys, some of which were the character dolls of the *Young England* series, *My Little*

Henry Hughes
Mr Golliwog

Territorial, *Our Little Dreadnought* (boy and girl) and *Dutch Boy and Girl*. In 1914 the new lines included 'leg style' Eskimo dolls, as well as skirt style and baby bunting Eskimos with celluloid faces and plush bodies. In 1924 the series included new *Folly Dolls* in Scottish, Irish and Welsh costumes and by 1925 there were over 400 styles of dolls including *Mr. and Mrs. Golliwog*, which looked very similar to the Atlas and Star variety, but the clothing was more realistic and not sewn together in one piece as with Star and Atlas. *Mr. Golliwog* had a short striped jacket, shoe button eyes, a stitched mouth, full trousers, a fur wig and a white shirt and tie.

Leven Bears

In 1891 the company Leven & Sprenger was founded in the town of Sonneberg, Germany. By 1910, the firm was making teddy bears for the American market under the name H Josef Leven. So successful was the enterprise that by 1912 the firm employed ten office staff and a hundred and fifty workers, making it one of the largest toy firms in the town. In 1923, an employee, Mr. Fred Engel became a partner and later president of the firm. Later, he bought the remaining part of the company and as the sole proprietor, appointed his daughters, Dorle and Hildegard as joint owners. After World War II the firm fell within the state of East Germany and by 1972 the family were expropriated and the Leven Co. became state owned. In 1990, with the fall of Communism, titles and buildings were returned to the Engels, the legitimate owners. Dorle Engel had married Rolf-Gerhard Hermann in 1951 and they

had fled to the west in 1953. Recently both Dorle and Hildegard decided that the firm would be continued by Hermann-Spielwaren GmbH, Coberg.

During the 1920s the Leven firm had produced their 'golliwog' dolls and today Hermann has introduced two replicas of the 1925 Leven golliwog, thousands of which had been exported to America and England at that time.

Merton Toys (Dean's)

A subsidiary company of the Dean's Rag Book Co, Merton included golliwogs in their range of dolls. In 1954 a brightly coloured rayon plush golliwog was produced. It was 19 inches high with rolling disc eyes, a mohair wig, red torso, yellow arms, blue legs, red feet and two blue rayon buttons. In the early 1960s the firm introduced a golliwog riding a tricycle.

Merton golliwog riding trike, 1960s

Made in the same style as the Dean's golliwogs of 1930, its legs would go up and down pedalling busily while a chime on the front wheels produced a tinkling note. It was dressed with a white bow tie, red and white striped trousers, a blue jacket and yellow waistcoat. The eyes were the plastic unmoving lock-in type and the tricycle was blue and red with blue and red wheels.

Replica Leven Bears, 1994

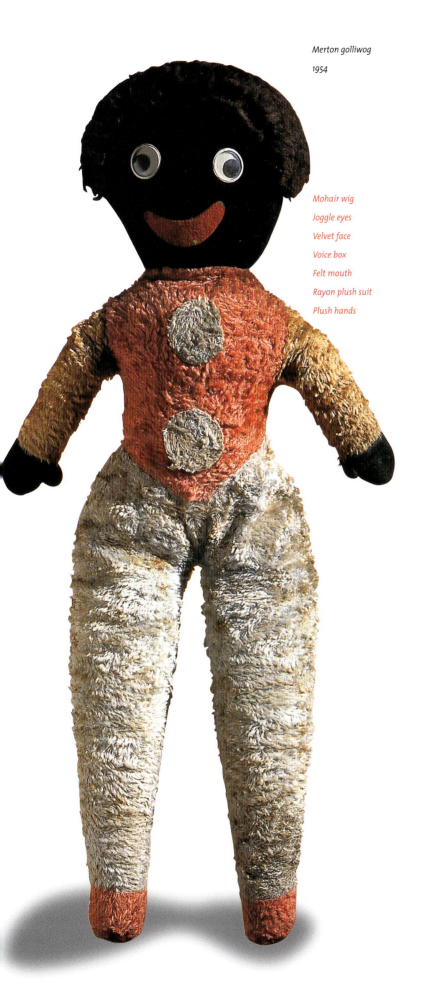

Merton golliwog

1954

Mohair wig

Joggle eyes

Velvet face

Voice box

Felt mouth

Rayon plush suit

Plush hands

The Nisbet Co.

The Nisbet Co. was formed in 1953 when Peggy Nisbet designed a 7 inch doll of Queen Elizabeth II to commemorate the Coronation. Other dolls followed and by 1956 the limited company was founded. The firm continued to produce many historical characters, and still makes quality dolls today.

Nisbet golliwog

Mostly double-knit

17¹/₂ inches high

H Schelhorn & Co.

Manufacture of the Teiltoy line began after the family left Sonneberg for England in 1935. A doll-making family, they started producing glass eyes for other firms such as Palitoy in Leicester. The firm made pottery dolls out of the clay Heinrich Schelhorn received in 'pug' form from the Stoke-on-Trent area. In 1945, Heinrich obtained a patent for an artificial eye for dolls and helped to produce dolls for the Ottnebergs of Derby, with his artistic heads.

Gai Golli, 1973

Golliwogs were made by the firm in the 1970s. One model was the *Gai Golli*, a minstrel golliwog soft doll which was musical and held a guitar. He wore striped trousers, a polka-dot bow tie and had hard plastic lock-in eyes. By the 1980s the firm produced vinyl plastic dolls like *My Baby Love* and *Jeanette*, a dressing doll outfit.

Sieve Sunlight & Co.

Only in business for a few years around World War I, this firm at Crescent Works, Chapel Street, Salford, Manchester, was a maker and exporter of toys and dolls. In 1915, its range included stuffed dolls made of printed fabrics, soldier and sailor dolls and golliwogs. The celluloid-faced dolls, composition head, china head and unbreakable jointed dolls, were introduced in 1917 and by 1919 the firm was producing high class and medium priced dolls with jointed appendages and glass eyes.

Star Manufacturing Co.

In business from 1887 with the factory in Cubitt Town, London and with offices at 29 New Oxford Street, London, this firm manufactured and exported dolls and toys. Both composition and stuffed dolls were produced along with baby dolls sporting porcelain heads. The 1965 golliwogs were almost identical to the Atlas golliwogs of the same period. Some of the Star golliwogs had white gloves and an array of patterned and coloured trousers, while the Atlas dolls had only black hands and chequered trousers. Star dolls also had colour variations in their jackets and ties, while Atlas golliwogs only used red for their jackets and light blue for the string tie. The eyes were of the same shoe button type used during this period.

Star Manufactuing Co.

golliwog

Steiff

Born in Giengen Germany in 1847, Margarete Steiff fell victim to polio at an early age. She was confined to a wheelchair and learned to sew to earn a living. Aged 30, she founded the Felt Mail Order Co. producing felt clothing and by 1880 she was selling stuffed felt toys. Fritz, her brother, helped her run the business, which flourished to become the Felt Toy Co. in 1893. By 1897, the firm employed ten workers at the factory and thirty home workers.

The company progressed when her nephew Richard Steiff joined the firm after he finished art school. His Bar 55 PB, (a string-jointed bear) was such a success in New York, that Hermann Berg (of the wholesale firm, George Borgfeldt and Co.), ordered 3,000. This was the start of the Steiff teddy bear industry. The firm sold 12,000 bears in the first year and won many awards for its creations and by 1907, Steiff had sold 975,000 bears. In 1905, the firm became Margarete Steiff GmbH. She was the owner and her nephews were directors, with 1,800 home workers and 400 factory employees when the firm was at its peak.

Around 1911, the firm produced its first and only golliwog called *Gow*, in various sizes, from 12 to 19 inches. There were jointed dolls and there was a roly-poly version with detachable arms and legs. Metal snaps held the limbs together.

After two world wars, Steiff resumed its status as the leading teddy bear maker. Even today few can equal a Steiff product. The firm has reproduced many of the early editions, but has not repeated their *Gow* or made any other golliwogs.

The Gow golliwog

12-19 inches high c.1911

Mohair wig

Felt face & hands

Shoe button eyes, felt backing

Formed nose

Felt mouth, jacket & trousers

Ribbon tie

Cotton shirt

Brass buttons

Black shoe buttons

Leather feet

Clifton Toy golliwogs
1954

E Westbrook golliwog, 1967

WG Sofdol golliwog
Foam filled, two sizes
Safe-lock eyes
1966

Nylo-Puff golliwog
36 inches high
Foam filled, washable
1964

A Codeg line by Cowan de
Groot Ltd, The Jolly Golly
A dancing figure who twirls
his cane while moving.
Fur wig, cane, 1952

Unidentified golliwogs

At 28 inches, this golliwog was manufactured some time between the 1940s to early '50s, possibly by Fondle Toys. The wig is synthetic, the facial features are painted, the body is of linen with velvet feet, a waxed cotton face, a wood-wool stuffed head and flock stuffed body. I have not seen another doll like this, and I am likely not to.

Painted eyes, nose & mouth
Rayon tie
Linen buttons, jacket & trousers

Short pile wig
Stitched eyes
Stitched nose
Stitched mouth
Cotton sheet
Felt shirt
Felt trousers

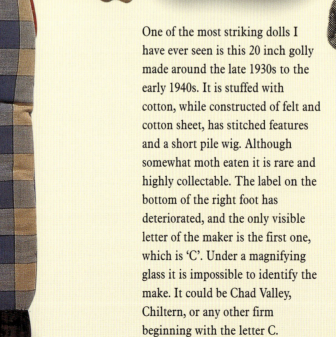

This golliwog is stuffed with kapok. The eyes are not original, the wig is mohair, while the face and body are of a sateen and cotton type fabric. The clothing is of velveteen, the shirt is cotton. Made around 1930s, it is a very rare doll indeed. It resides at the Bethnal Green Museum of Childhood.

One of the most striking dolls I have ever seen is this 20 inch golly made around the late 1930s to the early 1940s. It is stuffed with cotton, while constructed of felt and cotton sheet, has stitched features and a short pile wig. Although somewhat moth eaten it is rare and highly collectable. The label on the bottom of the right foot has deteriorated, and the only visible letter of the maker is the first one, which is 'C'. Under a magnifying glass it is impossible to identify the make. It could be Chad Valley, Chiltern, or any other firm beginning with the letter C.

Khaki helmet

Fur wig

Linen button eyes

Attached nose

Rolled attached mouth

Brass buttons

Khaki fabric

Khaki belt

Khaki puttees

Feet – inner linen layer

Hands – black outer

cotton layer

These golliwogs were made around 1907, before the Steiff golliwog. They are very well made, stuffed with cotton and covered with two layers of fabric, a rabbit fur wig and attached nose and mouth. The torso is simply made, with the arms and legs attached. By the year 2007, these golliwogs will be 100 years old and could last another 300 if they are properly looked after.

Fur wig

Linen button eyes

Attached nose

Rolled attached mouth

Linen dress & belt

Double layers of cotton

on face and body

This is an extremely desirable golliwog. Not only is it one of the earliest, but it wears a British khaki uniform which would also interest collectors of military memorabilia. The uniform resembles that worn during the Sudan campaigns. All of these early golliwogs are the most sought after.

Although these early British gollys are not made with the quality materials of a Steiff doll, they are no less collectable or valuable.

Fur wig
Linen button eyes
Attached nose
Rolled attached mouth
Attached bow tie
White linen shirt
Brass buttons
Linen trousers
Double cotton layers
on face & body

Golliwog
Manufacturer unknown
(one of those listed opposite)
c.1907

(Below) A Little Mother postcard by Raphael Tuck dated 1911.
Two of the golliwogs depicted in this postcard (left & centre in the girl's arms) are featured on this page

Golliwog
Manufacturer unknown
Cotton filled
Fur wig
Partly hand stitched
15 inches high
c.1907

Postcard, c.1908 depicting girl holding a golliwog similar to those shown here

"Of all my toys there is one,
of which the people laugh and jest
But he is the dearest of them all,
my Golliwog is best."

Golliwog
Manufacturer unknown
Wood wool & cotton filled
Linen outer layer
Arms & legs attached to torso
c.1906

Fur wig
Shoe-button eyes
Formed nose
Sewn mouth
Linen shirt & jacket
Brass buttons
Linen trousers

Golliwog
Manufacturer unknown
(Missing collar & tie)

Fur wig
Shoe-button eyes
Applied nose
Stitched cotton mouth
Oiled linen cloth
Shell buttons
Cotton jacket & trousers

Golliwog
Manufacturer unknown
Foam filled
28 inches high
c.1970s

Synthetic yarn wig
Felt eyes & mouth
Sailcloth face & body

This doll was on sale at Peter
Jones in London. Out of my
entire collection, it is the only
doll with a name. I call it
Spider, not only because of its
long arms & legs, but after I
purchase it, a spider crawled
out of its wig!

Black girl doll
British
Manufacturer unknown
Cotton filled
15 inches high
c.1960s

Pile wig
Joggle eyes
Felt mouth
Cotton face & body

British golliwog

Manufacturer unknown

Cotton filled

10½ inches high

c.1960s

Pile wig

Felt eyes & mouth

Cotton tie

Felt waistcoat

Cotton legs

Felt feet

Plastic golliwog

Manufacturer unknown

Made in Hong Kong

A troll-type doll

3½ inches high, 1980s

Golliwog

Manufacturer unknown

Could be Chad Valley or cheap

copy imported from Spain

c.1970s

Printed features

Ribbon tie

Sailcloth jacket

Cotton legs

Hand-crafted contemporary golliwogs

This is not a Steiff golliwog, but it is about as close as you can get. It is *'Mr. Gollywog'*, made by artist, Maria Schmidt. The tag on the jacket reads: *'The Charlestowne Bear/ Created By/Maria Schmidt'*.

Firmly stuffed, it is 22 inches in height and made entirely of felt, except for the shoe button eyes, ribbon tie, plastic buttons, brass buttons and synthetic wig. The arms and legs are jointed. With a limited edition of only 12 dolls, the value has soared.

Another, golliwog artist, Kathy Thomas has a line called, 'Golli and Me'. The dolls are limited editions, and the sizes and styles vary. Encouraged by the Upton 'Golliwogg' with a leather face, Kathy's gollies are made entirely of leather, suede, fur and brass buttons. The leather face has a formed nose, suede eyes and mouth with black button pupils. The remaining jointed body and clothing are suede. The wig is fur and with an edition of 125, the 5 inch dolls are rare.

Maria Schmidt golliwog

22 inches high

Kathy Thomas golliwog

Golly & Me

5 inches high

Kathy Thomas golliwog
Golly & Me
6½ inches high
Steiff influenced
Leather, suede, fur & felt,
with brass & plastic
buttons

The golliwog below is by bear artist
Barbara A Troxel, named *Bear Den Hollow*.
A most unusual doll, it is 6 inches in height,
with synthetic wig, glass eyes face mouth,
and claw-like hands. The nose is formed
and the jointed body is of velveteen, with
one brass button. Like the other dolls
created by artists it is very well made, but
what makes this golliwog so different is
the bear-like hump on the back and the
claw-like hands. It is a limited edition
and the head is jointed.

Right: Barbara A Troxel
Bear Den Hollow,
6 inches high

Golliwog
English
Foam filled
25 inches high
Straw hat & cane (missing)
1980s

Straw hat
Plush wig
Joggle eyes
Cotton tie
Plastic buttons
Sailcloth hands & feet
Felt mouth
Cotton shirt, jacket & trousers

Black make-up
1920s to 1960s

NEGRO BLACK by LEICHNER

Golliwog by Amy Brown
English, cotton filled,
15 inches high
1980s

Yarn wig
Felt eyes & mouth
Velveteen face & body
Felt jacket & waistcoat
Cotton trousers

Gabrielle Design Limited
English, cotton stuffed
23 inches high
c.1980

Plastic buttons
Cotton trousers & tie
Sailcloth body
Synthetic wig
Joggle eyes
Felt mouth
Lace cotton shirt
Felt jacket

Gabrielle Design Limited
English, cotton stuffed
23 inches high
c.1980

All felt golly
British
18 inches high
c.1990s

The first golliwog I ever saw
was made by an English doll
dealer in Los Angeles,
California, 1984

Yarn wig
Sailcloth face & body
Stitched eyes & mouth
Plastic buttons
Cotton trousers

COLLECTOR
TEDDY BEARS

Golliwog
Synthetic fabric
Plastic nose & eyes, pile wig
British, 1990s
(Sally Letham collection)

Golliwog
British, Jointed
8 inches high
Late 1990s
(Sally Letham collection)

Velveteen golliwog
18 inches high
Cotton filled
c.1940s

Home-made golliwog
English, 29 inches high
Cotton stuffed
c. late 1890s to early 1900s

Lambs wool wig
Velvet & canvas eyes
Velvet feet & hands
Cotton face
Wrapped red linen mouth
Chiffon shirt, tie & trousers

The only unhappy golliwog in
my collection

Home-made golliwogs

One of the drawbacks of home-made golliwogs is that they are difficult to date. A doll can be easily rendered with old fabric, buttons, fur, cotton and straw. The unscrupulous craftsman can recreate convincing dolls, which look as if they are pre-war golliwogs. My advice is to purchase such home-made golliwogs with a money back guarantee, stating that the doll is genuine and avoid dealers who will not give you this assurance.

Many collectors prefer home-made golliwogs and if you are one, choose those dolls which have an appealing character and are skilfully crafted. Basically, if you like it, buy it. But if you are puzzled about this type of doll, seek help from the experts.

Home-made golliwogs have a very strong appeal to American doll collectors because they often resemble early black folk dolls. So much so, that many enthusiasts are confused as to which is the golliwog and which is the folk doll. Therefore, many golliwogs are sold as folk dolls and vice versa.

Is there is difference? Yes and no. No, because the original golliwog was indeed a black folk doll made around 1880. Yes, because after the golliwog emerged, it took on a character all its own. In general, golliwogs have long, unkempt, black hair (unless cut by a previous owner) and clothing styled on the minstrel's morning dress coat and tie, usually brightly coloured. Its features are more whimsical in appearance with overly large eyes, red mouth and at times a bulbous or button nose. While many folk dolls look life-like, the golliwog looks more gnome-like.

Black folk dolls usually have closely cropped curly hair (female dolls have headscarves, long dresses with aprons and breasts); some have a piccaninny style with ribbons. The features include embroidered nose, mouth (sometimes with teeth) and oval shaped eyes. They are dressed in servile or poor clothing. There are always exceptions, so the more familiar you become with these dolls, the easier they will be to distinguish.

If you have a black soft doll, dressed a in brightly coloured morning coat, trousers and tie, and it is English made, it is most likely to be a golliwog. Few golliwogs were made in America and most of those which found their way there are from Britain. Girl golliwogs are scarce and even more difficult to identify.

Home-made golliwogs can fetch very high prices if they are truly early, but usually these dolls are cheaper than the manufactured variety. Made of scrap fabrics and other accessories they were stuffed with cotton, wood wool, or bits of scrapings. With no quality control, many were unhygenic and poorly designed and constructed. Still, to many collectors, they are no less desirable. But again, I stress, do not expect to make a heavy financial profit on home-made golliwogs; collectors nowadays are seeking the quality of well manufactured dolls.

Home-made golliwog

English

Cotton filled

12 inches high

c.early 1900s

Similar to the Florence Upton
Golliwogg of 1895

Fur wig (worn)

Leather face & nose

Linen button eyes

Velvet tie

Stitched mouth

Rayon waistcoat & trousers

Wool jacket

Cotton shirt

Shell buttons

Velvet body

Home-made golliwog

in night-dress

10 inches high

Cotton filled

One of the few girl versions

c.early 1900s

Fur wig

Formed nose

Stitched mouth

Heavy cotton face & body

Shoe button eyes

linen backing

Home-made black girl doll

English

Cotton stuffed

18 inches high

1950s

Home-made copy of
the Chad Valley, Woolly Wag
of the early 1920s
English
Cotton stuffed
11 inches high
1930s

Fur wig
Felt & yarn eyes
Stitched mouth & nose
Heavy cotton face & body
Felt waistcoat
Cotton jacket & trousers
Brass buttons

Home-made girl doll
English
18 inches high
Cotton stuffed

Human hair wig
Velvet & felt eyes
Felt mouth
Velvet face & body

Home-made golliwog

English

16 inches high

Cotton filled

1950s

Yarn wig

Felt eyes & mouth

Felt body & clothing

This doll is one of my personal favourites, because each time I see it, I can't help but laugh. The wild yarn wig, wide grin and round hips create an amusing picture

Home-made doll

Cotton stuffed

c.1960s to 1970s

(Dr Phipps collection)

Sailcloth body

Felt eyes & mouth

Cotton clothing

Home-made doll
18 inches high
Cotton filled
c.1930s-1940s
(Dr Phipps collection)

Fur wig
Felt mouth, eyes & feet
Rayon clothing

Home-made golliwog

English

18 inches high

c.1960s

Yarn wig

Felt & button eyes

Stitched nose

Rayon mouth

Stitched buttons

Cotton & rayon clothing

Cotton face & body

Many would be confused by this doll, but when you read children's books of the period, you will see gollies in this type of outfit, especially the bow tie

Home-made golliwog

20 inches high

Cotton filled

Velvet body

Felt eyes, mouth & feet

Rayon tie & jacket

c.1930s to 1940s

Home-made golliwog

20 inches high

Votton filled

Felt body

Satin shoes

Possibly a patterned kit doll

c.1930s to 1940s

Home-made golliwog

16 inches high

Cotton filled with velveteen

Felt shoes, eyes & mouth

c.1930s to 1940s

Home-made golliwog

Cotton filled

Satin, rayon & cotton clothing

Ccotton body

Felt eyes & mouth

Button centres

c.1990s

Home-made golliwog

Cotton filled

Felt & rayon body & clothing

c.1950s to 1960s

(Dr Phipps collection)

Home-made golliwog

16 inches high

Cotton filled

All cotton body

Cotton clothing

Felt eyes

c.1940s to 1960s

Home-made golliwog

14 inches high

Cotton filled

Rayon & sailcloth clothing

Rayon body

Felt eyes & mouth

c.1960s to 1970s

Home-made golliwog

15 inches high

Cotton filled

Felt & cotton clothing

c.1960s to 1970s

(Dr Phipps Collection)

Robertson's Jam Co.

It has been reported that while visiting America, one of the sons of James Robertson saw a child playing with a golliwog doll. I don't know if it was a golliwog or a black Negro doll, as golliwogs were not as well known as Sambo or Nigger dolls. I suspect it was most likely to have been a typical American 'Nigger doll.'

James acquired the doll and and brought it back to his family in England, who loved it so much, they decided that it should become the trademark for Robertson's products.

This trademark first appeared on Robertson's brochures in 1910, along with labels and various lists. The popularity of the golliwog was so great that the tin brooch was first introduced to the public during the early 1920's.

By 1928, the first enamel brooches were produced, made by Millers of Birmingham. A golliwog golfer was the first of the series, followed by a traditional (standing) golliwog. Next were the fruit brooches and in 1937-1939, a number of footballers and cricketers appeared.

In order to receive a brooch, a number of wrappers from various jars of preserves had to be submitted to Robertson's, who would send a brooch in return. Around 1940, production was halted to help with the war effort and later resumed, along with the brooch scheme. There were ten different brooches in all.

1. Small cup by Barratt's of Staffordshire, 1977

2. Promotional placard (as opposite), c.1940s-1950s

3. Traditional figure, 48 inches high, hardboard, c.1940s

4. Mug by Barratt's of Staffordshire, 1977

5. Toast rack by Silvercrane, 1980s

6. Christmas counter display, c.1960

These are promotional placards, made of painted hardboard. Each stands about 36 inches high. The wooden hardboard is very sturdy at 1/8 of an inch thick. Made circa.1940s to 1950s

They are a striking set. I have only seen one other figure and it was the trombone player. This is a very rare set, sought after by collectors of golliwog and advertising ephemera.

To get one brooch, ten 'paper tokens' (one per jar, under lid) had to be submitted. Around 1949, 50,000 brooches a month were being sent to customers. In the 1960s, tokens were placed behind the label. Pottery musician golliwogs were produced in 1963, comprising accordianist, bass player, clarinetist, drummer, guitarist, saxaphonist, trumpeter and singer, eight in all.

By 1969 a team of footballers was available and in 1971 the lollipopman was added. The footballers were discontinued in 1972 and all pottery production ceased in 1977, due to poor quality and poor distribution. In 1969, the weekly demand was 3,500-4,500 items.

In 1970, the token was placed on the jar label where it remained. Every year new designs were introduced to keep pace with topicality. In 1980, the scheme required collectors to submit five tokens plus 35p per brooch and was reduced again in 1985 to three tokens and 50p per brooch. Many other items were later included in the scheme, including, watches, caps, spoons, dolls, pens, mugs, T-shirts and puzzles. Each year Robertson's mailed out more than two million leaflets, which were updated anually, until the scheme finally ceased in the 1990s.

Note pad, fruit-scented, c.1980s

(Right) Plaster musicians and lollipop man, 1940s to 1950s

Manufacturers of golly brooches

All traditional golly brooches have the gazed eyes. Most have blue hands & red feet.

Fattorini	*Dark or light blue jacket, blue hands, red feet.*
Gaunt	*Black or red bow tie, normal or fat-curved legs.*
Greens	*Curly hair, black hands & feet or blue hands and black feet, chrome finish on brooch.*
Gomm	*Blue hands-red feet, red bow tie, chrome or brass finish.*
Toye	*Smaller brooch, large red tie, one hand in pocket.*
AWG, Charles Davis, Dingley	*Makers of the traditional brooches with light or dark blue jackets, blue hands, red feet, black hands,*
Firmin, Graham, Jewellery Metal Co.	*black feet, curly or smooth hair, red or black bow tie & chrome or brass finish.*
WC Lewis, Marples & Beasley	*There were variations in all of the companies.*
Melsom, Miller, Olympic, Reeves & Co.	

Manufacturers of musicians (figurines)

Wade	*Makers of the first musicians in porcelain. These figurines are higher in quality than the plaster types.*
	Also a hollow plaster type was produced later with the bandstand.

Other models

There were also plaster footballers (eleven) sporting the team number on the back. Later they were reproduced in plastic.

Lollipopman, (figurine) made in plaster, with paper 'STOP' notice glued to the sign.

Other plaster figurines include baseball player, boxer, cowboy, cricketer, fireman, guardsman, hockey player, mountie, nurse, pilot, postman, sailor, soldier, tennis player, traffic warden and the golly in-(armchair, beach buggy, car, jet & propellor plane).

Clocks & Watches

Wall Clock	*Round or square, wooden, (golly walking or head & torso), (large head & bow tie).*
Alarm Clock	*Oval shape with two bells.*
Watch	*Timex with white or yellow face, (digital, in blue, black, red or white).*

Cars, Lorries & Trucks

Dinky	*Guy lorry, red, No.919 Golden Shred, Van, fawn,Silver Shred.*
Matchbox	*Talbot Van, 1927 yellow with green, red or white wheels (Yesteryear).*
Lledo	*Van,red Golden Shred, Horse Drawn Van, Silver Shred.*
Matchbox	*Paisley Tram Golden Shred.*
Corgi	*Noddy's Car, No.801, with golly.*

Jean patches

These include: accordianist, balloonist, drummer, fisherman, footballer, guitarist, horserider, lollipopman, motorcyclist, racing driver, saxaphonist, skateboader, tennis player, yatchsman & Championship World Hot Air Balloon 1977

1. Toddler's chair, 1960s

2 & 3. Silvercrane teapots, 1980s

4. Silvercrane salt & pepper shakers, 1980

Robertson's badges were first introduced in the early 1920s. It is not known who the makers were, but the first badge was made of bakelite, which was die-cut with a fastening pin attached at the back. These badges are extremely rare. The next badge was made of tin with the front and back punched out, jointed and painted. The hair was a strip of fur wrapped around the head and glued. These badges were smaller than those which were to follow. The jacket was red, trousers blue and the shirt white. These badges are also rare.

Tin brooch, 1920s

During the early 1930s the tin badges became metal brooches with enameled coloured details on the front and the maker's name on the back. This is the style most familiar to collectors today, although the earliest examples of this style are very difficult to obtain. The first enameled brooches were made by Miller of Birmingham. These first enamels were the yellow waistcoat type, having the logo *Golden Shread* printed on the torso front. This style had several variations.

Around 1934, Robertson's also offered their fruit design brooches, which could be obtained by sending three labels, (two of which had to be pertinent to the jam of choice). The brooches were delivered to the customer on a card stating, *The World's Best Marmalades* and were packed in a cardboard box. Each brooch would represent one of the six types of fruit and each type would have the face of the golly in the die-cut design. These brooches were enameled with colours to coincide with each type of fruit.

The early years

Golfer Golly early 1930s

Miller	Golfer Golly brooch with opened legs & feet
	Golfer Golly brooch with metal cross piece joining feet
	Waistcoat with pockets & face with interlined lips
	Waistcoat without pockets & face with interlined lips
	Standard lips
	Standard strolling golly without enamel on a metal sphere
	Standard strolling die-cut golly without enamel
	(Numbers 6 and 7 may not have been circulated)

Fruit brooches 1934

Miller	Blackcurrant
	Bramble
	Lemon
	Orange
	Raspberry
	Strawberry

Footballer Golly 1937

Miller	Red & white ball, feet & hands of metal
	Red & white ball, black feet & white hands
	Green & white ball, feet & hands of metal
	Light blue & tan ball, black feet & white hands
	Light blue & white ball, black feet & white hands
	Black & white ball, feet & hands of metal
	Dark blue & white ball, feet &hands of metal
	Dark blue & white ball, black feet & white hands
Greens	Dark blue & white ball (ball a little smaller)
Melsom	Dark blue & white ball, feet & hands of metal

Miller Golfer Golly brooch, 1930s

Miller Fruit brooch No.4, 1930s

Miller Footballer Golly brooch, 1930s

1. Dinky Toys, Guy van in Golden Shred livery, 1958

2. Counter display, 1930s-1950s. Missing label. (Dr Phipps' collection)

3. Kilncraft Coloroll mug, 1970s

4. Infant's chair, 1960s

5. Cereal bowl, 1980s

6. Fabric backpack, c.1980s

1

2

3

THE JOLLY GOLLI

4

6

5

Around the time of the coronation of Queen Elizabeth, three differerent labels would get you a Coronation Golly Brooch, with a golliwog saluting at attention, sporting a Union Jack on his chest and standing on an oval base.

Also at this time, the footballer, hockey and tennis gollies were on offer. The hockey golly had a green enameled crosspiece joining black enameled feet and white enameled hands.

By 1937, the footballer golly came in many varieties from different manufacturers. The Miller Company produced eight styles over a two year period.

Around the same time, the cricketer gollies were introduced in numerous poses and produced by different manufacturers. There was the Miller version which had the metal foot crosspiece; Melsom's had white hands and the Graham brooches had a rounded metal foot crosspiece with plain metal feet and hands. Then there were the various club cricketer brooches representing all the counties of Great Britain as well as other countries like Australia. All of these were the yellow waistcoat type, made pre-World War II. As before, there were variants as well as some un-issued models. Two girl golly types remained un-issued.

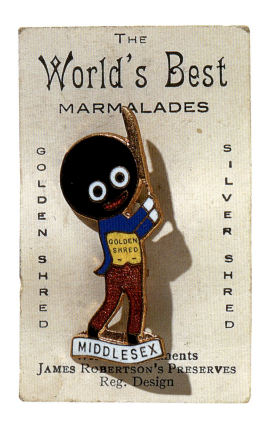

Robertson's tin, 1980s

Above: cricketer brooches

on backing cards, 1930s

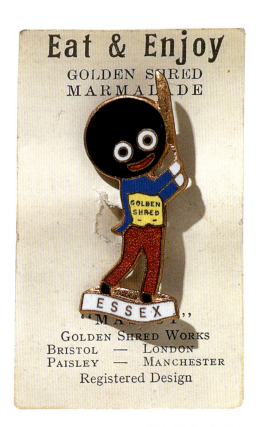

Right: Selection of cricketers

and bagpipe players, 1930s

Bagpipes Golly post-World War II

Miller	Standard gold bag.
	Smaller eyes & mouth.
	Bagpipes no enamel.
	Red bagpipes.
	Green bagpipes.
Fatturini	Dark blue, large mouth, mouth piece on right.
	Dark blue, small mouth, mouth piece on right.
	Dark blue jacket, large mouth, mouth piece on left.
	Light blue jacket.
F & S. of	Dark blue jacket, small mouth, mouth piece on left.
Birmingham	Light blue jacket.
	All of the above with Golden Shred.
No logo	Fatturini
on bag	F & S
	F & S. dark blue jacket
	Marples & Beasley light blue Jacket
	Richard Gomm
	REV & Gomm GS
	REV Gomm

Cricketer Golly post-World War II

Cricketers have centered eyes & lowered eyes, with differences
in the crosspiece at the feet & colours of hands & feet

Miller	Red feet & blue hands. Eyes either lowered or gazed.
	Legs bridged with metal & the feet crosspiece
	is either rounded on both ends or on right.
Gomm	Centered eyes, blue or black hands & red or black feet.
	Feet crosspiece either pointed at both ends
	or flat at both ends. Jacket is light & dark blue.
Fatturini	Centered eyes, blue or black hands, red or black feet,
	light & dark blue jacket, brass metal between legs.
Marples	Centered eyes, black hands & feet,
& Beasley	heavier & shorter leg.
JR Gaunt	All have lowered eyes, blue hands & red feet
	These are known variations in all makes.

1. Fatturini

2. Gomm
3. Fatturini
4. Fatturini
5. Fatturini

6. Fatturini
7. Miller
8. Gomm
9. Gomm

10. Maples & Beasley
11. Maples & Beasley
12. Miller
13. Fatturini

14. Fatturini
15. Fatturini
16. Fatturini

Footballers post-World War II

Miller	Brooches can have centered or lowered eyes.
	The ball is either dark brown, brown, white or bake metal.
	Hands & feet are blue, red or bare metal.
	The hair can be curly and the legs crossed.
Fatturini	Brooches in this series all have gazed eyes.
	The balls could be orange, gold or light tan
	& the jacket is light or dark blue.
Gaunt	Centered eyes. Balls vary from gold, orange, brown,
	blue/white & plain white. The feet & hands are bare metal.
Reeves	Lowered eyes, white balls, high neck waistecats
	& metal feet & hands.
REV Gomm	Centered eyes, orange gold or brown balls
	& metal feet & hands.
Charles Davis	Centered eyes, gold, orange or brown balls or red smaller ball.
	V-neck waistcoat, red & blue feet & hands.
Marples	Centered eyes, brown, orange or gold balls,
& Beasley	dark blue jacket & metal feet & hands.

1. Miller
2. REV Gomm, 1985
3. REV Gomm, 1985

Golfers post-World War II

Miller	Lowered eyes, blue or black hands, red or black feet, V-neek waistcoat.
Fatturini	Lowered eyes, black & blue hands, black & red feet, light blue jacket.
REV Gomm	Lowered eyes, with blue hands & red feet.

REV Gomm

Guitarist post-World War II

Miller	Blue hands, red feet & lowered eyes. The guitar is green, legs are slender.
Fatturini	Red feet, blue or black hands & broad or plump legs.
	Green or brown guitars, light or dark blue waistoat & lowered eyes.
REV Gomm	Red feet, blue hands, slender legs & green guitars with lowered eyes.
Marples	Lowered eyes, red feet, blue hands, green guitars & slender legs.
& Beasley	

REV Gomm, 1985

ECL Tresor Verlas
plastic bank, 1990s

Robertson's plastic
counter display,
1950s

Hockey

Maker	Eyes	Feet	Hands	Hair	Jacket	Ball
Miller	Lowered	Red	Blue	Wavy & very wavy		
Fetturini	Lowered	Black or red	Black or blue	Smooth	Light & dark blue	
REV Gomm	Lowered	Black & red	Black & blue			Small
Marples & Beasley	Lowered	Red	Blue			

Scout

Maker	Eyes	Feet	Hands	Hat	Flag	Mouth
Miller	Centered		Black	Brown	White	Centred
Fetturini			Black	Tan	White	Off-centred
REV Gomm	Large gazed	Yellow or black	Black	Tan or green	Large logo	Short or wide
Marples & Beasley	Centered		Black	Tan	White	Centred

Skater

Maker	Eyes	Feet	Hands	Hair	Jacket	Mouth
Miller	Lowered & large	Red	Blue	Very curly		Centred
Fetturini	Lowered	Red	Blue		Light & dark blue	Normal & large
REV Gomm	Lowered	Red	Blue		Light blue	
Gaunt	Lowered	Red	Blue	Curly		

Tennis player

Maker	Eyes	Feet	Hands	Hair	Jacket
Miller	Lowered	Red	Blue	Smooth or curly	
Fetturini	Lowered	Black	Black	Smooth	Light or dark blue
REV Gomm	Lowered large & small	Red	Blue	Smooth	
Marples & Beasley	Lowered	Black or red	Black or blue	Smooth	Light blue
Reeves	Lowered	Black	Black	Smooth	

Fruits

Maker	Fruit	Fruit colour	Leaf colour	Logo
Miller	Lemon	Bright & pale yellow	Green	Normal & smaller
Miller	Raspberry	Red & scroll reads Robertson or Robertson's		
Fetturini	Lemon	Bright yellow	Green / defined veins	
Fetturini	Raspberry	Red & scroll reads Robertson		

Paper tokens

The white waistcoat brooches of the post war era continued through the 1950s into the early 1960s. In order to receive a brooch, during the post war years, one had to send in ten different paper tokens, shaped as golliwogs in various musical or sporting activities. These were placed behind the paper label and later under thc lids. Later still the tokens became part of the label so there are various sizes within the series, ranging from about 7.1 cm to 5cm. Other tokens include the Musician and Sportsmen group, which are about 5cm in height.

In the 1970s booches were still enameled but the overall design looked more modern. The waistcoats were unadorned by print, the eyes were glancing to the side and the yellow colour of the waistcoat was a richer, darker shade than the 1930s examples. Other variations exist, for instance, a 1970s cricketer with a white waistcoat. This 1970s style of brooches had many of the same characters represented.

Barratt dish & bowl, 1980s

Paper token styles

1. *Trad. golly holding jar, flat colours &* Robertson's Golden Shred *as logo.*
2. *Trad. golly, with arms raised & number '5' printed in centre.*
3. *Walking golly, holding jar, detailcd face & hands,* Golden Shred *on chest.*
4. *Trad. golly without jar, detailed hair & face. White print on red trousers.*
   a) *Same golly with* Robertson's Bramble Seedless.
   b) *Same golly with* Robertson's Mincemeat.
   c) *Same golly with* Silver Shred.
5. *Trad. golly, flat colours,* Robertson's Golliberry *on chest.*
6. *Trad. golly, flat colows,* Robertson's Golden Shred *on chest.*
7. *Black woman in hat, holding fan,* Robertson's Mincemeat *on apron.*

Musicians & sportsmen 1950s

Accordionist
Bagpiper
Cellist
Clarinetist
Drummer
Guitarist
Percussionist
Saxophonist
Trombonist
Violinist
Boxer
Cricketer
Foolbuller
Golfer
Hockey player
Lacrosse player
Rugby player
Skater
Skier
Tennis player

Sportsmen 1970s

Bagpiper
Cricketer
Footballer
Golfer
Guitarist
Hockey player
Lollipopman
Motorcyclist
Scout
Skater
Skateboarder
Tennis player
Traditional

Some of the brooches had no maker's name stamped on the back, such as the scout type which had a wide or narrow mouth or a white waistcoat. There is also a golfer which is different in style to other types.

The 1980s brought acrylic brooches. The range of characters increased immensely and varied in colours. There were no names printed on the back other than James Robertson & Son PM Ltd. or the back was unmarked entirely. Some of the brooches had no acrylic coating, when they were first distributed. There were the five fruit brooches – blackcurrant, lemon, orange, raspberry and strawberry – with the golliwogs' face among the leaves appearing larger than in the 1930's types.

Other characters include:
1. Ambulanceman
2. Football player (American)
3. Astrounaut – white or blue shirt, white collar
4. Bagpiper
5. Viota baker
6. Brownie
7. Butcher
8. Driver (Automobile)
9. Commemorative golly, light or dark blue coat with or without acrylic coating
10. Cowboy
11. Cricketer, dark or royal blue ball, small or large ball
12. Cycle rider, with or without acrylic coating
13. Dary player
14. Doctor
15. Engine driver
16. Fireman holds hose with long or short nozzle
17. Fisherman
18. Footballer, white pointed boots or black boots pointed or round toe, also dark blue jacket
19. Golfer, white, yellow or metal club, also yellow ball and tee
20. Guitarist
21. Jogger, pointed or square feet, also trousers with a red stripe
22. Lollipopman, long or short pole
23. Milkman
24. Motorcyclist, dark or light blue windshield
25. Mountie, light to dark shades on hats

26. Nurse, light or dark blue uniform
27. Policeman, traditional or bobbled helmet
28. Postman
29. Racing car driver
30. Sailor
31. Skier with and without acrylic coating
32. Snooker player
33. Standard
34. Tennis player, white or cream coloured large or small racket.

Again there can be other variations of any given character. There are also Special Promotional brooches which were produced in limited numbers. Some were acrylic or enamel, while others were in precious metal. In acrylic there was the *Bank it Bottle Bank*, *Cystic Fibrosis*, *HMS Crighton* and *Golly Club* varieties. The enamel models included a lifeboatman by Fatturini. The precious metal groups comprised:
1. *Viota Baker* in silver, with no colouring, joined arm holding spoon and in 9 carat gold, without colouring and die cut arm holding the spoon or with a diamond in the spoon.
2. *Fireman* with silver nozzle and no colouring. 3. *Traditional Golly*, silver and acrylic, plain silver and 9 carat gold with or without acrylic colour.

There can be variations in each style.

In 1985 the collector's enamels were offered in limited editions. Each style of the fruit brooches featured four fruit among the leaves with the scroll stating, *Robertson's Collector*. On these brooches the golliwog's face was larger than the fruit and had side glancing eyes. There were oranges with blue, white, red or yellow scrolls. The lemons had a white or black scroll.

Also in 1985 there was the *1940s Brooch Collection* – the white waistcoat reproductions. Made by REV Gomm, it was stamped 1985 on the back so as to not confuse collectors. It came as a boxed set and comprised the traditional golly, footballer, golfer, guitarist, hockey player and tennis player. The set came in a presentation box and minor variations were common. Separate chrome models also circulated, but they were not made by Gomm, nor were they sold as a set so are possibly unauthorised.

JR Gaunt made the *Special* brooches around 1987-1988, when Robertson's were bought by the Rank Organisation (Rank Hovis McDougall. Produced in limited numbers, they were gold plated and all had dark blue jackets. There was no printing on the back.
1. Traditional golly with black feet and hands The enamel is omitted on lapels and cravat
2. Pendant
3. Ice Skater
4. Tennis player – white hand and black feet

The 1990s acrylic brooches can be recognized by their round toes and very small pupils They can also have several variants – James Robertson and Sons printed on the back or no print at all. They varied in appearance from earlier brooches and include:
1. American footballer with blue & yellow stars
2. Astrounaut
3. Baseball player
4. Brownie
5. Cricketer
6. Doctor
7. Fisherman
8. Footballer
9. Fireman
10. Jockey
11. Juggler

Enamel brooches
1960s to 1990s

1990s acrylic brooches continued:

12. Arabic golly
13. McGolly, black or white sporran and tassle
14. Nurse
15. Policeman
16. Racing driver
17. Skatebaorder
18. Skier
19. Surfer
20. Tennis player
21. Traditional

There is also a special *Father Christmas* promotional brooch made for Robertsons' staff.

Golly balloon badges

In the late 1970s and early 1980s, during the balloon rallies in which Neil Robertson had an interest with his tour *Golly Balloons*, the firm sold a series of very high quality enamel badges. Some were full bodied gollies, while others were just the head with a basket attached. The public edition was the balloon with white border stating, '*World Hot Air Balloon Championship, Castle Howard, York 1977*'. The background was the 'world' in blue enamel. The crews' version had a red border and yet another version had a white basket, red bow-tie and silver finish. These were made by Gomm. Variations were:

1. Golly 3/4 front view
2. Golly front view
3. Golly combination of three balloons and one front view figure standing on the right side or centre
4. Golly balloon, eyes glancing right or left
5. A quadruple balloon golly

Variations of finish also exist; the golly balloon badges came in silver, chrome or gold. There were also the encircled balloon badges of enamel with a blue or white background, with other variations in colours and styles.

Golly pendants

Also during the late 1970s and early 1980s pendants of different golly characters were produced, including:

Traditional Golly

Head	Smooth or curly
Eyes	Large or small glancing sideways
Waistcoat	White or yellow
Metal	Chrome or silver with enamel

Large silver enamel pendants
1. Traditional Golly
2. Tennis player, still or action with ball/racquet
3. Golfer
4. Footballer with blue-white or red-white ball
5. Skater

Metal pendants
1. Golly, stamped in square, round or oval metal

Acrylic pendants
1. Traditional Golly
2. Nurse

Button badges

Gaunt made many of these badges, while others have no makers name printed. Other badges were created such as the various slogan buttons:

1. *I'm Golly Buy me*
2. *Get it in glass*
3. *I'm a Golly Collector*
4. *I have seen the Golly Balloon*
5. *We just love Marmalades*
6. *50 Golden Years1930-1980*
7. *By Golly Buy British*
8. *Gollicrush Lemon Drink*
9. *Gollicrush Orange Drink*
10. *We have seen the Golly Balloon*
11. *Robertson's Preserves*
12. *Golly it's good*
13. *We just love Robertson's Marmalades*
14. *Jumping Golly on silver or gold background*
15. *I've joined the Golly Club*

Necklace, 1980s

Golly jar lids

The lids came with a full figure golly, torso golly or *Join the Golly Club* which you could adapt into a badge.

Golly figures

Initially, made of porcelain by Wade, the musician figures included:

1. Accordionist
2. Cellist
3. Clarinetist
4. Drummer
5. Guitarist
6. Saxophonist
7. Trumpeter
8. Singer
9. Bandstand

Later solid plaster models were produced. Finally hollow plaster models were offered as a re-issued group. The porcelain figures are very difficult to find, while the plaster models can still be seen at markets, fairs and shops.

There was also a team of eleven footballers in plaster with the team number on the back. These were later re-issued in plastic. The lollipopman is found in plaster with applied or painted sign. This model can also be found in plastic. Other plaster characters inolude:

1. Boxer
2. Cowboy
3. Cricketer
4. Footballer
5. Guardsman
6. Hockey player
7. Baseball player
8. Fireman
9. Lollipop
10. Mountie
11. Nurse
12. Pilot
13. Sailor
14. Postman
15. Soldier
16. Tennis player
17. Traffic warden
18. Golly in beach buggy, jet, propellor plane, chair or car

Brooches, badges, buttons and other items offered by Robertson's during the 1980s and 1990s are so numerous that it is near impossible to make an extensive verification of all these pieces. The following is but a small list, to give collectors some ideas in checking on their various items.

Clocks

1 Wall clock with golly torso
2 Wall clock with golly head
3 Wall clock with traditional golly figure
4 Wall clock, square made of wood
5 Alarm clock with double bell

Watches

1 Digital watch, blue, red, black or white
2 Watch – yellow face
3 Watch – white face (tirnex)

Cloth patches

These are on white or yellow background.

1. Traditional golly
2. Acordianist
3. Baloonist
4. Drummer
5. Fisherman
6. Footballer
7. Guitarist
8. Horserider
9. Lollipopman
10. Motorcyclist
11. Racing driver
12. Saxophonist
13. Skateboarder
14. Tennis player
15. Yatchsman
16. Balloon Championship 1977
17. Traditional shaped golly

Key rings

1. Rectangular metal, with black golly pressed into the metal
2. Plastic – traditional golly
3. Clear plastic – racing driver
4. Coated – baseball player
5. White back – walking golly

Toy trucks, lorries and vans

1. Large red truck by Dinky. Guy Lorry No. 919 *Golden Shred*
2. Yellow Talbot van, 1927, *Silver Shred* by Matchbox Y5 *Models of Yesteryear* with green wheels, red wheels or white trim wheels
3. Lledo D6 red *Golden Shred* van
4. Dinky – tan *Silver Shred* van
5. Lledo – horse drawn *Silver Shred* van
6. Matchbox – Paisley tram, *Golden Shred*

Tableware

Robertson's and other companies made many golliwog tableware items. Variations in all of the categories and the items are legion, as each offer leaflet could contain nearly thirty items.

Silvercrane

The mugs featured sporting or musical characters and came in two styles; one with smaller eyes.

Large eyed mugs

1. Traditional golly
2. Bass player
3. Cricketer
4. Drummer
5. Footballer
6. Golfer
7. Guitarist
8. Tennis player
9. Tuba player

Small eyed mugs

1. Footballer (American)
2. Cricketer (with eap)
3. Golfer (with bag)
4. Footballer (English)
5. Skateboarder
6. Tennis player

Other items

1. Butter dish – table tennis (2 gollies)
2. Cheese dish – skier
3. Egg cup – drummer or sailing club
4. Milk jug – bongo player
5. Sugar bowl – pianist
6. Teapot – cricketer or arm forming spout
7. Toast rack – motorcyclist or traditional

1. Robertson's golly watch, 1980s

2. Golly watch by Presta, made in Israel, moving eyes, 1970s

3. Goden Shred Die-cut poster, c.1940s

4. Book by Giles Brandreth, illustrated by Sara Silcock, 1980s

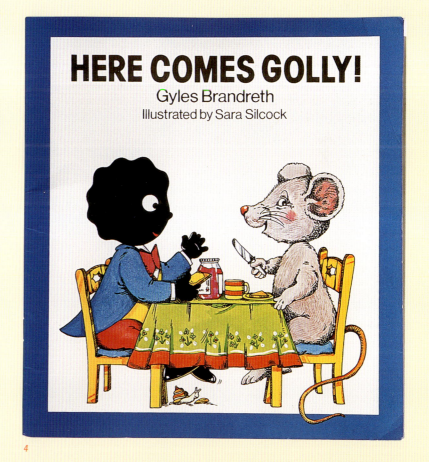

Robertson's printed rag golly
Foam filled
16 inches high
Features printed on cloth
1980s
(Sally Letham collection)

Robertson's Nurse golly
Foam filled
Detachable hat & apron

Many of the golliwog items issued by Robertson's were for various incentive promotions. Dolls like these are but only a few examples. Sadly today, having bowed to public pressure, the company no longer promotes its products with the much loved golliwog. Bye Golly!

Anne Wilkinson golliwogs
Made of synthetic pile
10 inches high, c.1980s

Robertson's golly
Foam filled
34 inches high
& smaller sizes
1980s

Conclusion

I have written this book to inform and to entertain, but I would like to think that it has prompted every reader to think more deeply about the effect that those black stereotypes created by white artists and designers have had on people's attitudes, and the barriers they have built to hinder the development of mutual respect and understanding.

The book raises a number of questions about the place of the golliwog in children's folklore, which the reader may wish to consider, such as:

Is the golliwog a visual metaphor for Black subservience? Is the golliwog a toy we regard with affection or is it an object of mild fun and ridicule for young inhabitants of the nursery? Should the golliwog, Sambo or any minstrel-type imagery be on sale? Is it desirable for Blacks and Whites to collect these items? Is this imagery suitable for white children in their formative years?

The impact of stereotypes on social attitudes

Over the years, I have campaigned vigorously on human rights issues and the rights of black people. I have been fortunate enough to visit and reside in many different countries, as an ordinary citizen, and I have encountered individuals, some of whom perceive Blacks as equals. However, it is easy to recognise that the majority still have had their views tainted by centuries of negative propaganda perpetrated by so-called Western civilisation, regarding black people as second class citizens.

Even in the twenty-first century, Blacks are still tarred with the same brush. Generally they continue to find they are regarded as academically inferior, more prone to drugs, crime, alcohol and laziness. With no real power in the media or newspapers, black people have little or no control over how they are perceived.

Restraint in a hostile society

Blacks are still considered to be the lowest order of society, nominally free, but economically enslaved. However, black people are reversing this process, by first taking pride in their true history and culture. They are beginning to move on, rebuilding their confidence by recognising the contributions they are continuing to make to civilisation. Understanding how far you've come, puts into perspective how far you can go.

It has been a long, hard struggle, but black heroes are now emerging in all areas of society, particularly in the arts and sport, where they naturally excel. Their example must continue to reach back to help those less fortunate, persuading our youth to cast aside centuries of prejudice they have endured from white domination. There's no quick fix to repairing the damage created by centuries of hate and ridicule, but to integrate fully, our black youngsters must reclaim their self-esteem and learn to respect others, unencumbered by negative icons of the past.

Should golliwogs be permitted?

In a free society it's difficult to prohibit sales. If people disagree with a product, they have to learn to deal with it in a mature and adult way. A ban infringes on artists' rights to express their ideas freely. I have no objection to this, unless such expressions become exploitative or stereotypical. For many years this was the case and Blacks were all viewed in this light. Nowadays things are changing and more positive black images are available and more and more black people find nothing negative in many of these beautiful abstract images, which are based on their culture and heritage.

Should Blacks or Whites collect these items?

Everyone has their own reasons for collecting and we are all entitled to that. Many Whites as well as Blacks find these images striking, and others find that the golliwog and Sambo figures induce fond memories. I see no harm in this.

Are these representations suitable for children's literature?

Again I believe in free expression, so I have no problem with golliwogs or black children being cast as characters in children's books or on TV programmes, as long as they are are positively represented. Just as white kids are portrayed in a more naturalistic design, young Blacks should also be depicted in this manner.

The image of a golliwog is likened to that of a clown. For many years black people were, and still are, depicted as grotesque stereotypes, while in the same picture their white counterparts, often women, were shown in a more flattering light. To erase prejudice, all people must be represented in a fair and unbiased manner, but will it happen?

Florence Upton and the Golliwogg

The Golliwogg series of books, published around the turn of the 20th century, is a landmark event in the annals of children's publishing. It was the first major series to feature a golliwog and being so, must have been an extraordinary experience for its young readers. There are many that feel Florence and Bertha Upton had very positive messages to convey to youngsters in their Golliwogg series, not least, the accord that existed between the black Golliwogg and the white Dutch Dolls. However, I believe that the Uptons and others, like Helen Bannerman and Enid Blyton, were products of racist Britain. There are those who say that the Golliwogg was not intended to be an insulting icon towards black people. But I say, how could it not be when the original doll was a representation of an American black butler or minstrel?

In the Upton books, *Golliwogg at the Seaside* and *Golliwogg in the African Jungle* examine how Florence depicts the black people in the seaside hotel as well as the African tribe. The natives look very much like the Golliwogg in appearance, especially to young developing minds, because they are drawn in the same stereotypical manner. Why do the African tribesmen attack the Golliwogg even though he resembles them? Well, the authors followed the racist British Empire doctrine of the day, that Africans were savages who would kill any outsiders, even white women (the Dutch Dolls) or those Blacks who were so-called 'civilised'. Notice also in Bertha's verses, at times the Golliwogg is referred to as a 'dog' or some other awful name (a derogatory term used by Whites to deal with under-performing servants), yet the book was for children's consumption. Yes there was a message for youngsters in each book but there was also a less favourable depiction of blacks people.

Changing views

First, I must inform anyone that views these images as 'negative', there is nothing negative about black people's features or colour. For centuries Western nations have encouraged the idea that a darker pigmentation equated to inferiority, buffoonery, evil, deceit and laziness. Yet, Whites loll around under the hot sun to 'get some colour!' After becoming somewhat 'orange or hot pink' they boast of being black, brown or tan. Today, super-models arch their backs to emphasize their derrières, film and TV stars wear padding to accent the buttocks, and fulsome lips are now highly desirable. Blacks were called savages when they wore little clothing on the plains of Africa. Yet when it is hot in the West the first thing many Whites do is remove their clothing.

After noting these actions by Whites, Blacks have now turned the perceived opinion of the golliwog and Sambo imagery around. In the USA, while some are still unsure, many black people see these images as beautiful or positive. Personally, I only object when a black caricature is paired with a natural-looking white person. Otherwise I view them as I would African art within its abstract form, unity of line/colour/pattern and beauty. Africans often portray themselves with coal black skin, red mouths and large white eyes. They deem this style as beauteous. As more Blacks begin to glorify and appreciate their physiognomy they gain in self-confidence and grow less likely to detest golliwog and Sambo type imagery. In fact, many black artists now interpret their work using these representations.

The effect of the Golly in Robertson's advertising

It is perhaps not surprising, that the Robertson Jam Co. decided to adopt the golliwog as a logo at the time they did. It was a familiar and popular image which appealed to children – who incidentally, loved jam! And although in latter years it has caused controversy, I do not feel that it was necessary for the company to have bowed to popular pressure and sacrificed the 'Golly', after so many years. Although, it was right for Robertson's to have long since removed the epithet, 'wog' from their marketing, so as not to offend ethnic minorities within the country. 'Wog' is a derogatory term used to insult or outrage, not dissimilar to the term 'nigger'.

The golliwog and American advertising

Even in America advertisers have updated images such as, Aunt Jemima and Uncle Ben in effort not to offend anyone. As Blacks become more economically and socially emancipated, stereotypical images and labels begin to lessen. Still, there are other stereotypes remaining which indeed need to be addressed. Each golliwog toy and illustration has its own personality, so it is quite difficult to have a favourite, especially with so many items around. American artists tend to favour the dolls with noses, which is apparent within their designs.

The golliwog – my impressions as a collector

As one examines this book, what becomes clear is that the golliwog has been and still is one of the most controversial of children's toys. Though nowadays it is not as popular as its playmate the teddy bear, golliwogs are no less important in the history of children's playthings. Of all the items which I collect, (including carousel animals, tin toy autos, Art Deco items, classic cars, American jukeboxes and black memorabilia, golliwogs are my personal favourite. From the moment I first saw these dolls, books and toys, I was overwhelmed by the variety of styles and designs. It is no wonder, that many thousands of children over the years found the golliwog so appealing.

Index